Fall, 1986 – the year of the bullet –

To my daughter, Lori

"The Happy Gardner"

Love,

Mother

May this book be of some help. Heaven knows you'll need all the help you can get!

"The lesson I have thoroughly learnt, and wish to pass on to others, is to know the enduring happiness that the love of a garden gives".
George S. Elgood, "Cleeve Prior: Sunflowers".

The
Making of a Garden

Gertrude Jekyll

*An anthology of her writings,
illustrated with her own photographs and drawings,
and watercolours by contemporary artists*

Compiled and edited by
Cherry Lewis

Antique Collectors' Club

© 1984
The Antique Collectors' Club
World copyright reserved

Revised 1985

ISBN 0 907462 52 9

British Library CIP Data
Jekyll, Gertrude
  The making of a garden
  1. Gardening
  I. Title   II. Lewis, Cherry
  635′.092′4   SB455

Published for the Antique Collectors' Club
by the Antique Collectors' Club Ltd.

Printed in England by Baron Publishing, Woodbridge, Suffolk

Introduction

The selections in this anthology of Gertrude Jekyll's writings are not necessarily the "best" in the sense of being the most practical for today's gardening enthusiasts. Indeed to attempt to make a selection on such lines would be to do a grave injustice to this remarkable woman, to whom the making of gardens was more than its practicalities.

This is in no way to detract from her constructive advice for it, in turn, reflects that inventive nature by which she was able always to put her own gardening experiences to practical ends.

Her early training at art school, and subsequent ventures into the worlds of wood carving, gilding, silver work and embroidery, had all played their part in shaping her strong, and single-minded views on design, form and the use of colour in gardens — views to which Miss Jekyll attached so much importance that no apology is made for the fact that they are repeated throughout this book.

The art school training also, no doubt, strengthened the power of observation with which she had been blessed from childhood. Ironically, this great strength lay partly in her weak eyesight: ... "The will and the power to observe does not depend on the possession of keen sight. For I have sight that is both painful and inadequate ... but the little I have I try to make the most of, and often find that I have observed things that have escaped strong and long-sighted people".

The progressive myopia meant that, at about the age of fifty, she had virtually to abandon her much-loved artistic activities. For many others, such a blow would mean a slowing down, a drawing back; for this mentally alert and physically energetic woman, it seemed to increase her enthusiasms and perceptions, and must quite certainly have led to the channelling of her abilities into an area of creativity which was not totally dependent on keen eyesight: the creation and control of her own garden; the designing of other people's gardens; and writing fluently about her experiences and observations in both.

Although she had for some years been contributing articles on gardening to magazines and newspapers, her first book, *Wood and Garden,* a collection of notes and thoughts which had originally appeared in *The Manchester Guardian,* was published in 1899 when she was fifty-six. Twelve more books followed during the next twenty-five years and it is from these, together with *A Gardener's Testament* (another collection of articles and notes for various journals) published posthumously in 1937, that this anthology, illustrated with her own black and white photographs and drawings, is made.

In making the final selection my aim was to go for "observations" which would not only entertain those who delight in reading about the heart and

soul as well as the maintaining of a garden; but also enthuse those who feel they want to but never quite can "get down to their gardens", for surely it is impossible to read Miss Jekyll without feeling spurred on? One reason for this, I suspect, is that she never makes a mystery of gardening matters; her approach is straightforward, down-to-earth; she will not be a slave to the garden or its plants, and is constantly searching out ways in which growing things can be made to adapt to her garden pictures.

A few pieces have only marginal connections with gardening ("Trees and honeysuckle", p. 50, and "People and practices", p. 70, for example); but they *had* to be included, for they so well characterise Gertrude Jekyll's perceptive, imaginative and sympathetic nature.

Since she wrote, times have changed: many of the plants referred to are no longer commonly seen or available; the classification of plant names is a continuous process of alteration; gardens have shrunk in size and gardening help in quantity. Yet to edit out all "anachronisms" would mean losing much that is quintessential Jekyll as well as much of the period charm. In fact, what is really remarkable is that so many of Miss Jekyll's writings still have relevance today.

Here then is a rich legacy of gardening lore, its delights, disasters, its pleasures and practicalities. The whole encompassed by her *bon mots:* "I have often noticed how surprisingly blue is the north side of a white goose"; her sense of humour: "One does not want to be every other day tinkering at the dahlias"; her good advice: "In all kinds of gardening where some kind of beauty is aimed at the very best effects are made by the simplest means"; and above all by her modesty and generosity: "I lay no claim either to literary ability, or to botanical knowledge, or even to knowing the best practical methods of cultivation; but I have lived among outdoor flowers for many years, and have not spared myself in the way of actual labour, and have come to be on closely intimate and friendly terms with a great many growing things, and have acquired certain instincts which, though not clearly defined, are of the nature of useful knowledge. But the lesson I have thoroughly learnt, and wish to pass on to others, is to know the enduring happiness that the love of a garden gives".

Cherry Lewis
Suffolk, 1984

"There are thousands of little girls in England, and small boys too, who would not only delight in working in a play-house, but who would in after years visit it again with delight... The pretty lady in the picture has brought out her work to the old play-house, and is trying to think herself a child again".

"When I used to make picnic fires... I always took a pair of bellows, and made it a point of honour to have the kettle boiling within five minutes of lighting the fire... I had always great delight in watching and feeding the fire at the garden burn-heap. I have the same pleasure in it now that I am old. It is such a clean, tidy, satisfactory way of getting rid of all the rubbish".

Of gardens

My own young days

Well do I remember the time when I thought there were two kinds of people in the world — children and grown-ups — and that the world really belonged to the children. And I think it is because I have been more or less a gardener all my life that I still feel like a child in many ways, although from the number of years I have lived I ought to know that I am quite an old woman. But I can still — when no one is looking — climb over a five-barred gate or jump a ditch. This was no doubt because my place in the family came in the middle of four boys; two brothers older and two younger. I had no girl companions, for my only sister was seven years older, so that we were not much together. It was therefore natural that I should be more of a boy than a girl in my ideas and activities, delighting to go up trees, and to play cricket, and take wasps' nests after dark, and do dreadful deeds with gunpowder and all the boy sort of things.

But when my brothers went to school I had to find my own amusements. There was a dear old pony Toby and the dog Crim, and we three used to wander away into the woods and heaths and along all the little lanes and by-paths of our beautiful country.

Soon I came to notice the wild flowers and wanted to know about them; but had no one to tell me till I was given a capital book that you will hear about presently; but I had got to know them as friends long before I could find out what their names were.

"A grand place for gudgeons. We used to catch them both with a rod and with a round dip-net, and sometimes had them fried for tea".

"The island was a sort of enchanted land ... and here the moor-hens built and brought out their broods of lovely little round black-velvet chicks".
Thomas Mackay,
"Evening — Hampton Lucy".

The old home, not very far from where I live now, had biggish spaces of garden and shrubbery and two ponds — one a large mill-pond covering some acres; and three streams, so that I was always watching the ways of water. Where one quick-running stream, after tumbling down in a cascade, ran into the mill-pond, was a grand place for gudgeons. This pond had a large island near the upper end, but no bridge. In our earlier years we had no boat, but belonging to the house was a set of brewing tackle, and among its items a beer-cooler. This is a wooden thing about five feet long and three feet wide, with sides eight or ten inches high, like a large shallow box or tray. My father had this taken down on the pond for something that was to be done near the pond edge, and we children surreptitiously used it as a boat to make perilous journeys over to the island... The island was a sort of enchanted land. It had some great poplars growing on it, and a tangle of undergrowth. Some of this came down and dipped into the water, and here the moor-hens built and brought out their broods of lovely little round black-velvet chicks. On the fringe of the island were the grandest lady ferns I have ever seen, and in its depths I first found the curious plant twayblade.

Where another of the streams, a slower one, came into the pond, was a fringe of the beautiful water forget-me-not. I never can forget — how could I, when it is just as keen to this day! — my delight in the pure blue of this sweet little plant, with its clean-looking bright green leaves, and its faint scent that I used to think like the small quiet smell of the little wild pansy that you find in cornfields among the stubble.

* * *

I was born in London: we came to live in the country when I was nearly five years old. Among the clearest of my recollections of London are some of grass and flowers. We lived in Grafton Street, close to Berkeley Square. When it was too hot to walk in the Green Park we borrowed the key at Gunter's and played in the square garden... How well I remember the smell of the mown grass. To this day the scent of cut lawn grass is the smell of that square garden. It was long before the days of mowing machines, and I remember seeing the man sweep up the grass that he had cut in the early morning. When short grass is cut with the scythe it is always done in the early morning, because when it is wet with dew it stands up better to the edge of the blade.

When we walked in the Green Park earlier in the year I was attracted by the dandelions, and wanted to bring them home to the nursery. But our nurse, Marson, for some reason of her own, did not like dandelions. She always said they were Nasty Things, and though I looked at them longingly and sometimes picked one to smell, I don't think I ever brought them home. But dandelion also remains with me as a London smell.

* * *

"We children surreptitiously used [a beer-cooler] as a boat... It was very naughty indeed — it was strictly forbidden, and was really dangerous, but mercifully we came to no harm".

Great was my pride and delight when I was first given a garden of my own, to do just what I liked with. It was in a long-shaped strip of ground notched out of the far end of the shrubberies of the big home garden, between them and a

"Some day you will grow up, and perhaps have a big garden of your own, and if you have learnt to know a lot about it when you were little, it will make you fit to take charge and say how things are to be done".
Mary Hayllar, "Helping gardener".

"There can be no doubt that the proper place for our shoes and stockings is on or near a garden bench".

"I used always to think that a grown-up wheelbarrow was a very comfortable thing to sit in when you were tired".

rising hedge-bank... In the spring we had primroses and forget-me-nots, yellow alyssum, white arabis and aubrietia and a few patches of the common double yellow daffodil... For summer flowers we had monkshoods — a plant I should never now put in a child's garden, because it is so poisonous. Then lupins and columbines, with annual larkspurs and pot marigolds, and some of the delicious old garden roses — damask roses and cabbage and moss roses and white pinks.

*   *   *

Later I was given another bit of ground close by. It was more a general messing-place than a garden, though I grew some lettuces and radishes and mustard and cress, and did a great deal of work that had not much result, but was absorbingly interesting to the solitary worker... On one side there was a space of about nine feet between the laurels, and here I made my hut... I had read somewhere about making walls of wattle and clay, and had found a place where there was a little clay, but it was some way from my garden and in a swampy place, difficult to get at. So after digging one or two of my little barrowfuls and making a great mess of myself, so that I was not very well received in the schoolroom afterwards, I gave it up, and my hut remained a hut of branches only — in fact a sort of skeleton arbour.

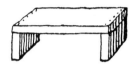

"The only furniture [in my hut] was a stool I made of some bits of board. The construction was not good, and it always wobbled when I sat on it, but I soon found out how to sit very carefully so as to avoid a collapse".

Johns' "Flowers of the Field"

My first knowledge of garden plants came through wild ones. Some one gave me that excellent book, the Rev. C.A. Johns' "Flowers of the Field". For many years I had no one to advise me (I was still quite small) how to use the book, or how to get to know (though it stared me in the face) how the plants were in large related families, and I had not the sense to do it for myself, nor to learn the introductory botanical part, which would have saved much trouble afterwards; but when I brought home my flowers I would take them one by one and just turn over the pages till I came to the picture that looked something like. But in this way I got a knowledge of individuals... I always think of that book as the most precious gift I have ever received. I distinctly trace to its teaching my first firm steps in the path of plant knowledge, and the feeling of assured comfort I had afterwards in recognising the kinds when I came to collect garden plants.

*   *   *

By this time I was steadily collecting hardy garden plants wherever I could find them, mostly from cottage gardens. Many of them were still unknown to me by name, but as the collection increased I began to compare and discriminate, and of various kinds of one plant to throw out the worse and retain the better, and to train myself to see what made a good garden plant... And then I learnt that there were such places (though then but few) as nurseries, where such plants as I had been collecting in the cottage gardens, and even better, were grown.

Beginning and learning

Many people who love flowers and wish to do some practical gardening are at their wit's end to know what to do and how to begin. Like a person who is on skates for the first time, they feel that, what with the bright steel runners, and the slippery surface, and the sense of helplessness, there are more ways of tumbling about than of progressing safely in any one direction. And in gardening the beginner must feel this kind of perplexity and helplessness, and indeed there is a great deal to learn, only it is pleasant instead of perilous, and the many tumbles by the way only teach and do not hurt. The first few steps are perhaps the most difficult, and it is only when we know something of the subject and an eager beginner comes with questions that one sees how very many are the things that want knowing. And the more ignorant the questioner, the more difficult it is to answer helpfully... I think in such cases it is better to try and teach one simple thing at a time, and not to attempt to answer a number of useless questions... The real way is to try and learn a little from everybody and from every place. There is no royal road. It is no use asking me or any one else how to dig — I mean sitting indoors and asking it. Better to go and watch a man digging, and then take a spade and try to do it, and go on trying till it comes, and you gain the knack that is to be learnt with all tools, of doubling the power and halving the effort; and meanwhile you will be learning other things, about your own arms and legs and back, and perhaps a little robin will come and give you moral support, and at the same time keep a sharp look-out for any worms you may happen to turn up.

*   *   *

"It is no use asking me or anyone else how to dig... Better to go and watch a man digging, and then take a spade and try to do it". Sketch by Edwin Lutyens of Gertrude Jekyll, c.1896.

"I have learnt much from the little cottage gardens that help to make our English waysides the prettiest in the temperate world".
D. Woodlock, "On the Leam at Offchurch near Leamington".

"It seems to me that the duty we owe to our gardens and to our own bettering in our gardens is so to use the plants that they shall form beautiful pictures".
George Hughes, "A colourful array".

15

"Even in ordinary gardening there is almost too much to choose from. One of the modern French artists has described painting as l'art des sacrifices. *The best free gardening is also an art demanding constant restraint and a constant sacrifice, as well as the knowledge and keen discrimination that can choose ... what will serve best to make the intended garden picture".*

Some ladies asked me why their plant had died. They had got it from the very best place, and they were sure they had done their very best for it, and — there it was, dead. I asked what it was, and how they had treated it. It was some ordinary border plant, whose identity I now forget; they had made a nice hole with their new trowel, and for its sole benefit they had bought a tin of Concentrated Fertiliser. This they had emptied into the hole, put in the plant, and covered it up and given it lots of water, and — it had died! And yet these were the best and kindest of women, who would never have dreamed of feeding a new-born infant on beefsteaks and raw brandy. But they learned their lesson well, and at once saw the sense when I pointed out that a plant with naked roots just taken out of the ground or a pot, removed from one feeding-place and not yet at home in another, or still more after a journey, with the roots only wrapped in a little damp moss and paper, had its feeding power suspended for a time, and was in the position of a helpless invalid. All that could be done for it then was a little bland nutriment of weak slops and careful nursing

*   *   *

I have learned much, and am always learning, from other people's gardens, and the lesson I have learned most thoroughly is, never to say "I know" — there is so infinitely much to learn... Nature is such a subtle chemist that one never knows what she is about, or what surprises she may have in store for us.

Often one sees in the gardening papers discussions about the treatment of some particular plant. One man writes to say it can only be done one way, another to say it can only be done quite some other way, and the discussion waxes hot and almost angry, and the puzzled reader, perhaps as yet young in gardening, cannot tell what to make of it. And yet the two writers are both able gardeners, and both absolutely trustworthy, only they should have said, "In my experience *in this place* such a plant can only be done in such a way."

* * *

I have learnt much from the little cottage gardens that help to make our English waysides the prettiest in the temperate world. One can hardly go into the smallest cottage garden without learning or observing something new. It may be some two plants growing beautifully together by some happy chance, or a pretty mixed tangle of creepers, or something that one always thought must have a south wall doing better on an east one. But eye and brain must be alert to receive the impression and studious to store it, to add to the hoard of experience.

* * *

"Is it only an instance of patriotic prejudice or is it really, as I believe, a fact that no country roads and lanes in the temperate world are so full of sweet and homely pictorial incident as those of our dear England?"
Arthur Claude Strachan, "Cottage garden".

Often in choosing plants and shrubs people begin the wrong way. They know certain things they would like to have and they look through catalogues and order these, and others that they think, from the description, they would also like, and then plant them without any previous consideration of how or why.

Often when I have had to do with other people's gardens they have said: "I have bought a quantity of shrubs and plants; show me where to place them;" to which I can only answer: "That is not the way in which I can help you; show me your spaces and I will tell you what plants to get for them."

Many places that would be beautiful if almost left alone are spoiled by doing away with some simple natural feature in order to put in its place some hackneyed form of gardening.

*　　*　　*

There are many people who almost unthinkingly will say, "But I like a variety." Do they really think and feel that variety is actually desirable as an end in itself, and is of more value than a series of thoughtfully composed garden pictures?... So I try, when I am in a garden of the ordinary kind where the owner likes variety, to see it a little from the same point of view; and in the arboretum, where one of each of a hundred different kinds of conifers stand in their fine young growth, to see and admire the individuals only, and to stifle my own longing to see a hundred of one sort at a time, and to keep down the shop-window feeling, and the idea of a worthless library made up of odd single volumes where there should be complete sets, and the comparison of an inconsequent jumble of words with a clearly-written sentence, and all such naughty similitudes, as come crowding through the brain of the garden-artist (if I may give myself a title so honourable), who desires not only to see the beautiful plants and trees, but to see them used in the best and largest and most worthy of ways.

There is no spot of ground, however arid, bare, or ugly, that cannot be tamed into such a state as may give an impression of beauty and delight. It cannot always be done easily; many things worth doing are not done easily; but there is no place under natural conditions that cannot be graced with an adornment of suitable vegetation.

*　　*　　*

Ever since it came to me to feel some little grasp of knowledge of means and methods, I have found that my greatest pleasure, both in garden and woodland, has been in the enjoyment of beauty of a pictorial kind. Whether the picture be large as of a whole landscape, or of lesser extent as in some fine single group or effect, or within the space of only a few inches as may be seen in some happily-disposed planting of alpines ... or whether it is the grouping of trees in the wood by the removal of those whose lines are not wanted in the picture, or in the laying out of broad grassy ways in woody places, or by ever so slight a turn or change of direction in a wood path ... or for any of the many local conditions that guide one towards forming a decision, the intention is still always the same — to try and make a beautiful garden-picture.

*　　*　　*

"... some happily disposed planting of alpines".

If I have laid special stress upon gardening for beautiful effect, it is because it is the way of gardening that I love best, and understand most of, and that seems to me capable of giving the greatest amount of pleasure. I am strongly for treating garden and wooded ground in a pictorial way, mainly with large effects, and in the second place with lesser beautiful incidents, and for so arranging plants and trees and grassy spaces that they look happy and at home, and make no parade of conscious effort. I try for beauty and harmony everywhere, and especially for harmony of colour. A garden so treated gives the delightful feeling of repose, and refreshment, and purest enjoyment of beauty, that seems to my understanding to be the best fulfilment of its purpose.

"If I have laid stress upon gardening for beautiful effect, it is because it is the way of gardening that I love best, and understand most of, and that seems to be capable of giving the greatest amount of pleasure".

*   *   *

Let no one be discouraged by the thought of how much there is to learn. Looking back upon nearly thirty years of gardening (the earlier part of it in groping ignorance with scant means of help), I can remember no part of it that was not full of pleasure and encouragement. For the first steps are steps into a delightful Unknown, the first successes are victories all the happier for being scarcely expected, and with the growing knowledge comes the widening outlook, and the comforting sense of an ever-increasing gain of critical appreciation. Each new step becomes a little surer, and each new grasp a little firmer, till, little by little, comes the power of intelligent combination, the nearest thing we can know to the mighty force of creation.

And a garden is a grand teacher. It teaches patience and careful watchfulness; it teaches industry and thrift; above all, it teaches entire trust.

Planning and planting

The formalists are unjust when they assume that every path not in a straight line must therefore 'wriggle', and that any shaped or moulded ground must deserve such a term as an 'irrelevant hummock', or that, in general, gardening other than formal is 'vulgar'. It is not to be denied that there are wriggles and hummocks and vulgarities in plenty... But is is unfair to assume that these are in obedience to the principles of the free school. On the contrary, it teaches us to form and respect large quiet spaces of lawn, unbroken by flower beds or any encumbrance; it teaches the simple grouping of noble types of hardy vegetation, whether their beauty be that of flower or foliage or general aspect. It insists on the importance of putting the right thing in the right place, a matter which involves both technical knowledge and artistic ability; it teaches us restraint and proportion in the matter of numbers or quantity, to use enough and not too much of any one thing at a time; to group plants in sequences of good colouring and with due regard to their form and stature and season of blooming, or of autumnal beauty of foliage. It teaches us to study the best means of treatment of different sites; to see how to join house to garden and garden to woodland.

*   *   *

"If a garden lends itself to plantings of season by season ... there will then, throughout the summer, always be some one place that shows a complete and satisfactory garden picture".

"Even in London there are many opportunities for ornamental gardening ... such a place, intelligently planned, may be made into something delightful to look at". George S. Elgood, "Levens" (detail).

There is frequent complaint among horticultural amateurs to the effect that they cannot keep borders of hardy flowers well furnished with bloom throughout the summer. But in an ordinary garden it is quite unreasonable to expect that this can be done. It can only be done where there are the means of having large reserves of material that can be planted or plunged in the borders to take the place of plants gone out of bloom. Owners of gardens should clearly understand that this is so — acceptance of the fact would save them from much fruitless effort and inevitable disappointment. If a really good display is desired, it can only be conveniently done by restricting the season to a certain number of weeks — by devoting separate borders or other garden spaces to a definite time of year. If a border is planted so as to show a good garden picture through July, August and September, it will be quite as much as can be expected, and even then some dropping in of pot plants will be needed. But it stands to reason that the shorter the time in which the border is required to be ornamental, the better it can be done; and if a garden lends itself to plantings of season by season, or can be so arranged that such plantings can be carried out, there will then, throughout the summer, always be some one place that shows a complete and satisfactory garden picture, while the one that is to come next is showing early promise.

*   *   *

Even in London there are many opportunities for ornamental gardening — opportunities that have been almost entirely neglected. Nothing is more usual in a London house than that the back room on the drawing-room floor should look into nothing better than a dingy well between sooty walls. The prospect is so uninviting that the window is commonly screened by curtains, or, at best, by a few plants in pots. But such a place, intelligently planned, may be made into something delightful to look at from both the ground and the first floor. Then it is well to consider that, in days of increasing noise and disturbance from street traffic, these back-facing rooms have become the only places of refuge from the outer turmoil, and anything that will give them a pleasant outlook, with the light undimmed, is all the more to be desired and valued. Ways of planning will depend on structural capability, but even in the most difficult cases there will be found some way of bettering the prospect, while in the greater number some kind of pretty garden may be achieved. A few square yards of paving with borders next the walls, raised a few inches and supported and edged by a boldly moulded stone kerb, may have a planted setting of some of the hardy ferns and other foliage plants that will endure town conditions. Flowering plants bought in the market or from the coster's barrow are dropped in between and renewed when their beauty is past. At the far end, bounding the view from the windows there would be some distinct ornament, a raised vase or a *corbeille* of flowers, or the return of the border itself rising in two shaped tiers, or at best a well-designed wall fountain and basin. Figs, vines and Virginia creeper all do well in London, and would provide ample wall covering.

*   *   *

"There is no spot of ground, however arid, bare or ugly, that cannot be tamed into such a state as may give an impression of beauty and delight. It cannot always be done easily; many things worth doing are not done easily".
George S. Elgood, "Kellie Castle" (detail).

"At the far end, bounding the view from the windows there would be some distinct ornament, a raised vase or a corbeille *of flowers".*

"The whole question of the relation of vegetation to architecture is a very large one, and to know what to place where, and when to stop, and when to abstain altogether, requires much knowledge on both sides. The horticulturist generally errs in putting his plants and shrubs and climbers everywhere, and in not even discriminating between the relative fitness of any two plants whose respective right use may be quite different and perhaps even antagonistic. The architect, on the other hand, is often wanting in sympathy with beautiful vegetation. The truth appears to be that for the best building and planting, where both these crafts must meet and overlap and work together, the architect and the gardener must have some knowledge of each other's business, and each must regard with feelings of kindly reverence the unknown domains of the other's higher knowledge".

Left, Munstead Wood, Gertrude Jekyll's home designed by Edwin Lutyens; the approach through the wood. Below, the close connection of house and garden illustrated by an architect's drawing.

"Many years ago I came to the conclusion
that ... it is better to plant in long rather
than block-shaped patches. It not only has a
more pictorial effect, but a thin long planting
does not leave an unsightly empty space
when the flowers are done and the leaves
have perhaps died down. The word 'drift'
conveniently describes the shape I have in
mind, and I commonly use it in speaking of
these long-shaped plantings".

"As in all matters relating to design in
gardening, the good placing of plants in
detail is a matter of knowledge of an artistic
character. The shaping of every group of
plants, to have the best effect, should not
only be definitely intended, but should be
done with an absolute conviction by the hand
that feels the drawing that the group must
have in relation to what is near, or to the
whole form of the clump or border or whatever the nature of the place may be".

Even when a flower border is devoted to a special season ... it cannot be kept fully furnished without resorting to various contrivances. One of these is the planting of certain things that will follow in season of bloom and that can be trained to take each other's places. Thus, each plant of gypsophila paniculata when full grown covers a space a good four feet wide. On each side of it, within reasonable distance of the root, I plant Oriental poppies. These make their leaf and flower growth in early summer when the gypsophila is still in a young state. The poppies will have died down by the time the gypsophila is full grown and has covered them.

*   *   *

Delphiniums, which are indispensable for July, leave bare stems with quickly yellowing leafage when the flowers are over. We plant behind them the white everlasting pea, and again behind that, clematis Jackmanii. When the delphiniums are over, the rapidly forming seed-pods are removed, the stems are cut down to just the right height, and the white peas are trained over them. When the peas go out of bloom in the middle of August, the clematis is brought over. It takes some years for these two plants to become established ... but good gardening means patience and dogged determination. There must be many failures and losses, but by always pushing on there will also be the reward of success. Those who do not know are apt to think that hardy flower gardening of the best kind is easy. It is not easy at all. It has taken me half a lifetime merely to find out what is best worth doing, and a good slice out of another half to puzzle out the ways of doing it.

*   *   *

The careful gardener is always on the look-out for ways of making plants conform to his needs. Among various devices one of the most useful is the simple expedient of cutting back a tall plant in order to bring its flowers to the height desired. That excellent border plant campanula lactiflora ... grows to a height of anything up to six feet. Self-sown seedlings are apt to appear near an established clump. One of these had grown into a sturdy plant, but as it was too close to the front edge of the border it was cut down in June to about a foot above ground, and the result was a flowering mass about 2½ feet high. This cutting back does not seem to affect the time of blooming, though it might have been expected to retard it; but if done at the right time the cut-down plant keeps pace exactly with the taller uncut shoot. This useful shortening of height can be practised with several other plants, such as Michaelmas daisies.

*   *   *

Then there is the way of pulling down tall plants whose natural growth is upright. At the back of the yellow part of the border are some plants of a form of helianthus orgyalis, trained down ... it throws up flower-stalks from the axis of every pair of leaves. But other plants can be treated in the same way; the tall rudbeckia Golden Glow, and dahlias and Michaelmas daisies. The tall snapdragons can also be pulled down and made to cover a surprising space of bare ground with flowering side-shoots.

Colour in the garden

To plant and maintain a flower border, *with a good scheme for colour,* is by no means the easy thing that is commonly supposed.

I believe that the only way in which it can be made successful is to devote certain borders to certain times of year; each border or garden region to be bright for from one to three months ... For many years I have been working at these problems in my own garden, and, having come to certain conclusions, can venture to put them forth with some confidence.

* * *

I am strongly of the opinion that the possession of a quantity of plants, however good the plants may be themselves and however ample their number, does not make a garden; it only makes a *collection* ... and it seems to me that the duty we owe to our gardens and to our own bettering in our gardens is so to use the plants that they shall form beautiful pictures... It is just in the way it is done that lies the whole difference between commonplace gardening and gardening that may rightly claim to rank as a fine art. Given the same space of ground and the same material, they may either be fashioned into a dream of beauty ... or they may be so misused that everything is jarring and displeasing. To learn how to perceive the difference and how to do right is to apprehend gardening as a fine art.

* * *

"To apprehend gardening as a fine art ... is to place every plant or group of plants with such thoughtful care and definite intention that they shall form part of a harmonious whole".
Theresa Sylvester Stannard, *"Herbaceous borders".*

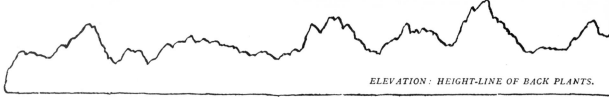

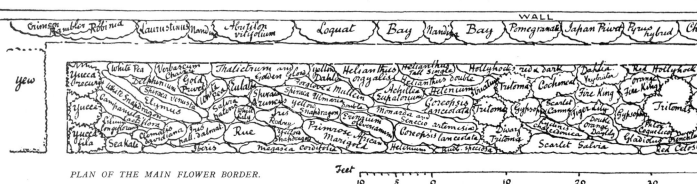

PLAN OF THE MAIN FLOWER BORDER.

Feet
10　5　0　　　10　　　20　　　30

Every year, as I gain more experience, and, I hope, more power of critical judgement, I find myself tending towards broader and simpler effects, both of grouping and colour. I do not know whether it is by individual preference, or in obedience to some colour-law that I can instinctively feel but cannot pretend even to understand, and much less to explain, but in practice I always find more satisfaction and facility in treating the warm colours (reds and yellows) in graduated harmonies, culminating into gorgeousness, and the cool ones in contrasts; especially in the case of blue, which I like to use either in distinct but not garish contrasts, as of full blue with pale yellow, or in separate cloud-like harmonies, as of lilac and pale purple with grey foliage. I am never so much inclined to treat the blues, purples, and lilacs in gradations together as I am the reds and yellows. Purples and lilacs I can put together but not these with blues; and the pure blues always seem to demand peculiar and very careful treatment.

*　　　*　　　*

The planting of the [main flower] border is designed to show a distinct scheme of colour arrangement. At the two ends there is a groundwork of grey and glaucous foliage — stachys, santolina, cineraria maritima, sea-kale and lyme-grass, with darker foliage, also of grey quality, of yucca, clematis recta and rue. With this, at the near or western end, there are flowers of pure blue, grey-blue, white, palest yellow and palest pink; each colour partly in distinct masses and partly intergrouped. The colouring then passes through stronger yellows to orange and red. By the time the middle space of the border is reached the colour is strong and gorgeous, but, as it is in good harmonies, it is never garish. Then the colour strength recedes in an inverse sequence through orange and deep yellow to pale yellow, white and palest pink; again with blue-grey foliage. But at this, the eastern end, instead of the pure blues we have purples and lilacs.

Looked at from a little way forward, for a wide space of grass allows this point of view, the whole border can be seen as one picture, the cool colouring at the ends enhancing the brilliant warmth of the middle.

*　　　*　　　*

"No means should be neglected or despised that will make the border handsome and effective..."

26

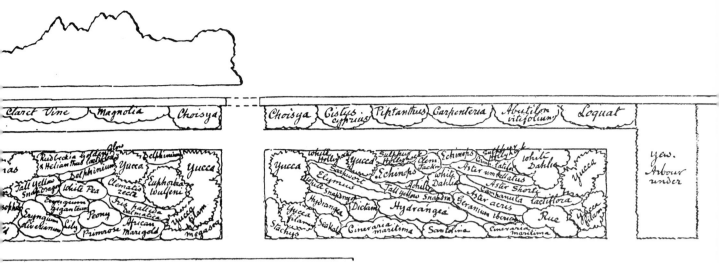

Claret Vine | Magnolia | Choisya | Choisya | Cistus cyprius | Piptanthus | Carpenteria | Abutilon vitifolium | Loquat

Yew. Arbour under

100

No one who has seen or carried out such a scheme, and whose desire it is to have the best effects that the flowers can give, will be contented with a haphazard mixture. Such an arrangement in harmonies is not only satisfying as a whole picture, but, though perhaps unconsciously to the observer, it follows natural laws relating to sight; for the cool and tender colouring is the best optical preparation for the splendour of the warmer masses, and, when the eye has had its fill of this, it receives a distinct sense of satisfaction when it comes again to the cool and restful colouring of flower and foliage. It is like passing from some shady place of half-light into the brilliant glow of hottest sunshine, and then, when this is almost too burning and oppressive, coming again to the quiet comfort of coolest shade and perhaps the sound of running or splashing water.

*   *   *

There is one matter that is commonly overlooked, but that makes all the difference between a border that is to be a picture of good colouring and one of lesser value. This is the provision of what may be called 'between' plants. For masses of colour, even if arranged in quite a good sequence, are only truly pictorial if between and among the colour groups there are other masses or accompaniments of neutral colouring... Especially among the plants of tender colouring there should be a rather full planting of grey foliage, such as rosemary, lavender, rue, phlomis, lyme-grass, clematis recta (out of flower), and, towards the front, lavender cotton, catmint, stachys and pinks. The effect of the plants of white and tender colouring is greatly enhanced by such a setting, while, when the border is surveyed as a whole, the advantage is quite unmistakable. Even with the permanent perennials, the bedding plants and the annuals, a border is apt, here and there, to show a place that might be better furnished. To remedy this it is well to have some plants in pots in reserve — hydrangeas, lilium longiflorum, lilium auratum and campanula pyramidalis are among the most useful — ready to drop in where they will make the best effect. No means should be neglected or despised that will make the border handsome and effective, and all such ways of doing it are so many spurs to further beneficent inventiveness.

*   *   *

"... and all such ways of doing it are so many spurs to further beneficent inventiveness".

27

It is rare to see, anywhere in England, plant-tubs painted a pleasant colour. In nearly every garden they are painted a strong raw green with the hoops black, whereas any green that is not bright and raw would be much better. This matter of the colouring of all such garden accessories as have to be painted deserves more attention than it commonly receives. Doors in garden walls, trellises, wooden railings and hand-gates and seats — all these and any other items of woodwork that stand out in the garden and are seen among its flowers and foliage should, if painted green, be of such a green as does not for brightness come into competition with the green of leaves. In the case of tubs especially, it is the plant that is to be considered first — not the tub.

* * *

Elsewhere I have written of the deplorable effect in the garden landscape of the glaring white paint ... that emphasises the ugliness of the usual greenhouse or conservatory. This may be mitigated, if the unsightly structure cannot be concealed, by adding to the white a good deal of black and raw umber, till the paint is of the quiet warm grey that for some strange reason is known to house-painters as Portland-stone colour.

Gardens of special colouring

It is a curious thing that people will sometimes spoil some garden project for the sake of a word. For instance, a blue garden, for beauty's sake, may be hungering for a group of white lilies, or for something of palest lemon-yellow, but it is not allowed to have it because it is called the blue garden, and there must be no flowers in it but blue flowers. I can see no sense in this; it seems to me like fetters foolishly self-imposed. Surely the business of the blue garden is to be beautiful as well as to be blue. My own idea is that it should be beautiful first, and then just as blue as may be consistent with its best possible beauty. Moreover, any experienced colourist knows that the blues will be more telling — more purely blue — by the juxtaposition of rightly placed complementary colour.

* * *

There is some curious quality, not easy to define, about flowers of pure blue, such as delphinium, anchusa, cornflower, and the useful dwarf lobelia, that demands a contrast rather than a harmony; for though in a blue garden the colouring can, with more or less success, be made to pass from the pure blues into those of purpler shades, such as those of the campanulas, yet it is a duller thing than if the pure blues only are used, with the companionship of something of white or pale yellow such as white or yellow lilies, white phlox or pale yellow snapdragon; or the creamy white of artemisia lactiflora or clematis flammula.

* * *

"Every year, as I gain more experience, and, I hope, more power of critical judgement, I find myself tending towards broader and simpler effects, both of grouping and colour".
George S. Elgood,
"The Pergola,
Great Tangley" (detail).

"Surely the business of the blue garden is to be beautiful first, as well as to be blue. My own idea is that it should be beautiful first, and then just as blue as may be consistent with its best possible beauty".
Beatrice Parsons, "Delphiniums".

"The grey garden is so called because most of its plants have grey foliage, and all the carpeting and bordering plants are grey or whitish. The flowers are white, lilac, purple and pink. It is a garden mostly for August, because August is the time when the greater number of suitable plants are in bloom; but a grey garden could also be made for September, or even October, because of the number of Michaelmas daisies that can be brought into use".

It is not the first time that attention has been drawn to the importance of grey and silvery foliage in the arrangement of flower borders for the late summer; but this aspect of gardening has of late aroused so much interest among amateurs, and such unqualified encouragement from artists, that some notes about its planting may be helpful to those who desire to make their gardens pictorially beautiful. The best season for such an arrangement is the six weeks during the months of August and the first half of September. It is unfortunate that these weeks coincide with the time when so many are away on holiday ... but there are many good gardeners who are at home and able to enjoy not the grey garden alone, but all the splendid border flowers whose best effect seems to culminate at just the same season.... Of these the most important in the grey garden are hollyhocks and dahlias, those whose colouring is right with the other flowers of purple, pink, and white, in the complete setting of silvery-white foliage that is the keynote of the grey garden's harmony... There are not too many pink flowers available, but among the best are some of the phloxes, especially the cooler of the pink-toned varieties, and one or two of the pale lilacs. It is best to avoid any pink flowers inclining to the salmon tints; the cool colours are better with the purple flowers.

*   *   *

In the green garden shrubs of bright and deep green colouring and polished leaf-surface predominate ... the flowers are fewer and nearly all white ... giving just a little bloom for each season to accompany the general scheme of polished and fern-like foliage. A little bloom of palest yellow shows in the front in May and June.

Colours of flowers

I am always surprised at the vague, not to say reckless, fashion in which garden folk set to work to describe the colours of flowers, and at the way in which quite wrong colours are attributed to them... Nothing is more frequent in plant catalogues than "bright golden yellow", when bright yellow is meant. Gold is not bright yellow. I find that a gold piece laid on a gravel path, or against a sandy bank, nearly matches it in colour; and I cannot think of any flower that matches or even approaches the true colour of gold, though something near it may be seen in the pollen-covered anthers of many flowers. A match for gold may more nearly be found among dying beech leaves, and some dark colours of straw or dry grass bents, but none of these when they match the gold are bright yellow.

*   *   *

Flowers of a full, bright-blue colour are often described as of a "brilliant amethystine blue". Why amethystine? The amethyst, as we generally see it, is a stone of a washy purple colour, and though there are amethysts of a fine purple, they are not so often seen as the paler ones, and I have never seen one even faintly approaching a really blue colour. What, therefore, is the sense of likening a flower, such as a delphinium, which is really of a splendid pure-blue colour, to the duller and totally different colour of a third-rate gem?

*   *   *

When blue is named ... what is meant is a perfectly pure blue, a colour that is perfect and complete in itself — that has no inclination whatever to a reddish or purplish tone. It means the blue of commelina, of salvia patens, of lithospermum and some of the gentians; of ipomœa Heavenly Blue, of anagallis Phillipsii, of anchusa and the best delphiniums, with the lighter blues of forget-me-not, omphalodes verna and nemophila. These, and a few others, may all be described as perfectly pure blues. They are none too many and are, therefore, all the more precious in garden use.

*   *   *

The term flame-coloured ... is often preceded by the word "gorgeous". This contradictory mixture of terms is generally used to mean bright scarlet. When I look at a flame, whether of fire or candle, I see that the colour is a rather pale yellow, with a reddish tinge about its upper forks, and wide wings often of a bluish white — no scarlet anywhere. The nearest approach to red is in the coals, not in the flame. In the case of the candle, the point of the wick is faintly red when compared with the flame, but about the flame there is no red whatever.

*   *   *

The terms bronze and smoke may well be used in their place, as in describing or attempting to describe the wonderful colouring of such flowers as Spanish iris, and the varieties of iris of the squalens section. But often in describing a flower a reference to texture much helps and strengthens the colour-word. I have often described the modest little iris tuberosa as a flower made of green

"Tritomas in the flower border... The flower spike is tall and of brightest colouring".

31

satin and black velvet. The green portion is only slightly green, but is entirely green satin, and the black of the velvet is barely black, but is quite black-velvet-like... Indeed, texture plays so important a part in the appearance of colour-surface, that one can hardly think of colour without also thinking of texture. A piece of black satin and a piece of black velvet may be woven of the same batch of material, but when the satin is finished and the velvet cut, the appearance is often so dissimilar that they may look quite different in colour.

*　　*　　*

What a wonderful range of colouring there is in black alone to a trained colour-eye! There is the dull brown-black of soot, and the velvety brown-black of the bean-flower's blotch; to my own eye, I have never found anything so entirely black in a natural product as the patch on the lower petals of iris iberica... The blotch of the bean-flower appears black at first, till you look at it close in the sunlight, and then you see its rich velvety texture, so nearly like some of the brown-velvet markings on butterflies' wings. And the same kind of rich colour and texture occurs again on some of the tough flat half-round funguses, marked with shaded rings, that grow out of old posts, and that I always enjoy as lessons of lovely colour-harmony of grey and brown and black.

*　　*　　*

Sage-green is a good colour-word, for, winter or summer, the sage-leaves change but little. Olive-green is not so clear, though it has come by use to stand for a brownish green, like the glass of a wine-bottle held up to the light, but perhaps bottle-green is the better word. And it is not clear what part or condition of the olive is meant, for the ripe fruit is nearly black, and the tree in general, and the leaf in detail, are of a cool-grey colour. Perhaps the colour-word is taken from the colour of the unripe fruit pickled in brine, as we see them on the table. Grass-green any one may understand, but I am always puzzled by apple-green. Apples are of so many different greens, to say nothing of red and yellow; and as for pea-green, I have no idea what it means.

*　　*　　*

Snow-white is very vague. There is nearly always so much blue about the colour of snow, from its crystalline surface and partial transparency, and the texture is so unlike that of any kind of flower, that the comparison is scarcely permissible. I take it that the use of "snow-white" is, like that of "golden yellow", more symbolical than descriptive, meaning any white that gives an impression of purity. Nearly all white flowers are yellowish-white, and the comparatively few that are bluish-white, such, for example, as omphalodes linifolia, are of a texture so different from snow that one cannot compare them at all. I should say that most white flowers are near the colour of chalk; for although the word chalky-white has been used in rather a contemptuous way, the colour is really a very beautiful warm white, but by no means an intense white.

I can remember when the only phloxes were white and a poor lilac... Nowadays we all know the beauty of these fine flowers, the large size of the massive heads and of the individual blooms; the pure whites, the good lilacs and pinks, and that most desirable range of salmon-rose colourings".
George S. Elgood, "Phlox".

Water in the garden

Happy are those who desire to do some good water-gardening and who have natural river and stream and pond, as yet untouched by the injudicious improver. For a beautiful old bank or water edge is a precious thing and difficult to imitate. If it is lost it is many years before its special features can be regained. But if the pond still possesses its own precious edge, and has its upper end half silted with alluvial mud, its great tussocks of coarse sedges, its groups of alders and luscious tufts of marsh marigolds, it is as a canvas primed and ready for the artist's brush.

"The beautiful Japanese water-loving iris... The best way to grow them in England is in the boggy margin".

*   *   *

Where there is a stream passing through the outskirts of a garden, there will be a happy prospect of delightful ways of arranging and enjoying the beautiful plants that love wet places... Where there are water forget-me-nots it would be quite enough to see them and the double meadow-sweet, and some good hardy moisture-loving fern, osmunda or lady fern... Close by the stream-side and quite out of view of other flowering plants should be a bold planting of iris ... the handsome Japanese kind... It is in varied colourings of white, lilac, and several shades and kinds of purple; but for this stream, where it is desirable to have the simplest effects, the single pure white alone will be best... The position of my garden, on a dry hill in the poorest soil, makes it impossible for me to grow them.

*   *   *

Of trees and bushes of the water-side, willows and poplars are the most important. The white willow (salix alba) becomes a good-sized tree. There are occasionally places where the weeping willow can be planted with good effect, perhaps for preference at the edge of small pools. But much more generally useful are the willows or osiers with highly-coloured bark, especially the cardinal and the golden osiers. In winter they quite light up the water-side landscape with their cheerful colouring, which is all the more brilliant if they are cut down every year; the young rods bearing the brighter bark. Nearly as bright in winter is the red dogwood, also willing to grow near water.

The poplars are the largest of the deciduous trees for the river or pond side or anywhere in damp ground. Grand great trees they are — the white, the grey, the black and also the aspen poplar; but grandest of all and most pictorial is the tall upright Lombardy poplar.

Sometimes nearly a straight line of these tall trees will occur near a river, and often have they been so planted with the very best effect; the strangely clear contrasting line of straight tall tree and level water being acutely accentuated when the one is reflected in the other.

*   *   *

"In the case of a wild forest pool ... it would be an ill deed to mar its perfection by any meddlesome gardening. The most one could do in such a place, where deer may come down to drink and the dragon-fly flashes in the broken mid-summer light, would be to plant in the upper ground some native wild flower that would be in harmony with the place ... but nothing that would recall the garden. Here is pure forest, and garden should not intrude. Above all, the water-margin should be left as it is... There are many places that call aloud for judicious planting. This is one where all meddling is forbidden".

"Many are the lovely plants that are not exactly marsh plants, but that like ground that is always cool and rather moist. In the wettest of this would be a plantation of primula denticulata, a grand plant indeed when grown in long stretches in damp ground at the edge of a hazel copse, when its luscious leaves and round heads of lilac flower are seen quite at their best... Two beautiful Indian primroses of a smaller size that also like a damp place, though less shade, are p. rosea [right] and p. involucrata Monroi; the latter seldom seen in gardens, though it is one of the most charming of hardy primulas".

"The way to enjoy ... beautiful things is to see one picture at a time; not to confuse the mind with a crowded jumble of too many interesting individuals ... but to follow a simple and clever arrangement of bold groups of suitable plants".
W. Tyndale, "Meadowsweet".

"*Not only does wistaria yield its masses of bloom almost unfailingly year after year, but its foliage is both graceful and handsome, and always looks fresh and clean... Wistaria though they grow fast when established, always make a long pause for reflection at the beginning of their new life's journey*".

Mildred Anne Butler, "Kilmurry: An upper window".

"The planted rill may be considered the invention of Sir Edwin Lutyens. The one in the garden at Hestercombe shows the most typical form. The wide paved ledges make pleasant walking ways; at even intervals they turn, after the manner of the gathered ribbon strapwork of ancient needlework, and enclose circular tanklets, giving the opportunity of a distinct punctuation with important plants".

"Water lilies ... are still better in a pond of moderate size, or even in one that has more the character of a large pool. If this has a near surrounding of wooded rising ground ... at such a distance as to shut in the scene and to promote stillness of the water surface, the pond will be a happy one for its lilies".

"The graceful primrose sikkimensis furnishing the margin of a pool... On the whole the Asiatic primulas are an easy race, well mannered, of good temperament, and never troublesome to manage, either in the more unconventional surrounding of the woodland or water-side where they are probably more at home".

Nothing is more significant of the great advance in appreciation of horticultural matters than the careful attention that is being given by architects to garden design. Twenty years ago the architect scarcely gave it a thought; now it closely engages his attention and stimulates his power of invention. And in no part of the garden is this more clearly shown than in the design and ornamentation of the varied accessories — pools, tanks, and fountains — that have for their purpose some delightful use of water ... the capital invention of the paved rill that can easily be stepped over, is gladly adopted and is freely used in varying fashion, always proving a charming addition to the interest of the garden... Both sight and sound of water are so pleasant that the tank may well be brought into immediate connection with the house; the paving of the near path or loggia only intervening. Here we may sit in shade and wonder at the beauty of the many-coloured water lilies fully opened to hottest sunshine, and watch the play of light and colour and reflection, ever changing throughout the day; and see how it all responds to the restraining discipline of good design.

*　　*　　*

An important matter in the appearance of all garden tanks is that the water should be kept at a high and constant level. Nothing looks much worse or more neglectful in a garden than a half-empty tank. The higher the level — consistent with a practical overflow — the better. It should be remembered that with a high level, reflections are the least broken.

*　　*　　*

Certain plants, and especially those that, like the water-lilies, have a very clearly defined character, seem able to give us their highest beauty in just certain circumstances. We have to find out the right kind of environment. Beautiful they are and must be in all ways, but one of the things most needful in good gardening is to study the plants and provide them with the most

"Nothing is more interesting than to plan and construct a combination of rock and water. Given perfectly bare ground, if only the needful supply of water and change of level are there ... there is no end to the combination of form that may be devised".

suitable sites and surroundings. Thus, delightful as the water lilies are in the margin of a wide lake, they are still better in a pond of moderate size, or even in one that has more the character of a large pool. If this has a near surrounding of wooded rising ground, not of trees overhanging the water, but at such a distance as to shut in the scene and to promote stillness of the water surface, the pond will be a happy one for its lilies... As in nearly all other gardening, if the best pictures are wanted, the simplest ways must be employed; for if too many kinds are mixed up or even used too close together, the best effect of the picture is lost. Thus if more than one colour or kind is to be seen at a time, it is best to put together gentle harmonies, as of white and pale yellow, or white and pale rose. Pale and deep rose also, with blush-white, will make a pleasant colour harmony.

"Here we may sit in shade and wonder at the beauty of the many-coloured water lilies fully opened to hottest sunshine, and watch the play of light and colour and reflection".
Lilian Stannard, "The lily pond".

40

Rock gardening

I have two small rock gardens, differently treated. The upper one leads from lawn to copse, and is made with a few simple parallel ridges of stone, clothed for the most part with small shrubs, such as gaultheria and Alpine rhododendron, with hardy ferns, and groups of two or three plants of conspicuously handsome foliage, such as saxifraga peltata and Rodgersia podophylla. The object of this one is to lead unobtrusively from lawn to copse, and at the same time to accommodate certain small shrubs and handsome plants with a place where they would do well and where I should wish to see them. The other little rock garden, between the lower end of the lawn and a group of oaks, has another purpose. It is absolutely artificial, and only pretends to be a suitable home for certain small plants that I love. A rock garden takes a great deal of skilled labour, and I can only afford it my own, so that its size is limited to little more than I can work with my own hands and see with extremely short-sighted eyes. Four broad and shallow steps lead down to the path-level; there is a long-shaped island in the middle, and sloping banks to right and left, all raised from the path by dry-walling from one to two feet high. The joints of the dry-walling are planted with small ferns on the cool sides, and with stonecrops and other dwarf sun-loving plants on the sides facing south... The various members of the mossy branch of the great saxifrage family are some of the most valuable of rock garden plants, and in a small place like mine can be well employed to give some sort of feeling of unity to what would otherwise be only a piece of floral patchwork, especially if the plants and their mossy setting are placed as much as possible in long drifts rather than in compact patches.

*   *   *

For the effectual destruction of any pictorial effect in a rock garden, no method of arrangement can be so successful as the one so very frequently seen, of little square or round enclosures of stones placed on end, with the plant inside conspicuously labelled. It always makes me think of cattle-pens in a market, and that the surrounding stones are placed prison-wise, less for the plant's comfort than for its forcible detention. And it leads to the stiffest and least interesting way of planting. If there are three plants they go in a triangle, if four, in a square, if five, in a square with one in the middle, and so on. For even if a little rockery be avowedly artificial, as in many cases it must be, it is better that its details should be all easy and pretty, rather than stiff and awkward and unsightly.

*   *   *

No rock garden should be without achillea umbellata in fair plenty. Even out of flower it is one of the neatest of plants, with its silvery foliage so deeply cut that the leaves are almost like double combs... There is no better plant for an informal edging, or for any alpine carpeting, in long pools or straight drifts; it delights in a hot place and, like many silvery-leaved plants, will bear a good deal of drought.

*   *   *

"Achillea umbellata ... with its bountiful heads of milk-white flowers, whose centres, dusky at first, change to a dull nankeen colour as the bloom becomes perfect".

My little rock garden is never without some stretches of the common thrift, which I consider quite an indispensable plant. Its usefulness is not confined to the flowering season, for both before and after, the cushion-like growths of sober greenery are helpful in the way of giving an element of repose and quietude to a garden-space whose danger is always an inclination towards unrest and general fussiness. And it should be cautiously placed with regard to the colour of the neighbouring flowers, for its own pink is of so low-toned a quality that pinks brighter and purer spoil it completely. I should say its best companions would be some of the plants of woolly foliage and whitish flower.

*　　*　　*

It has always seemed to me that when there is a very small space to be dealt with, as in the gardens of hundreds of small villas in the suburbs of London and other large towns, that to lay it out as a rock garden would be the best way of making the most of it. No doubt many clever owners of such houses have done it already, but others may not have thought of it, and though in a restricted area one cannot have large effects, yet there is no reason why one should not have well-designed ones, such as would be in perfect proportion and suitability of scale to the space at command; while such a little garden would admit of a much greater variety of forms of plant beauty than could be appropriately used in any other way.

*　　*　　*

Where water is available, and especially where there is a natural supply and a good fall in the ground level, the delights of the rock garden may be greatly increased... On a still summer day, nothing is more delightful, apart from the admiration of lovely plant and flower form, than to sit quite still and listen to the sounds of the water of the little rills. Their many voices may almost be likened to a form of speech, for in trying to convey in words the sensations received, we can only use those that apply to human vocal expression; for where the water runs between slightly impeding stones the sound is a kind of murmuring; where the path of the stream is wider and more shallow and set with many small pebbles it is a babbling, and where it passes rather quickly in steep descent through narrow, tortuous places the water has a sound of gurgling. And in all these there is a kind of musical note extending over a wide range, from a high-pitched bell-like tinkle to a deep, muffled sonority. It is only when it falls free, with the lesser splash or the heavier plunge, according to the volume that is delivered into the pool, that it loses the vocal quality and acquires a quite different, though always delightful, sound.

Wall gardening

Many a garden has to be made on a hillside more or less steep. The conditions of such a site naturally suggest some form of terracing, and in connection with a house of modest size and kind, nothing is prettier or

"It is one of the pleasures of the rock garden to observe what plants ... will serve to make pretty mixtures, and to see how to group and arrange them (always preferably in long-shaped drifts) in such a way that they will best display their own and each other's beauty; so that a journey through the garden, while it presents a well-balanced and dignified harmony throughout its main features and masses, may yet at every few steps show a succession of charming lesser pictures".

"The beautiful detail of structure and marking in such plants as the silvery saxifrages can never be so well seen as in a wall at the level of the eye or just above or below it; and plain to see are all the pretty ways these small plants have of seating themselves on projections or nestling into hollows, or creeping over stony surface . . . or standing like erinus with its back pressed to the wall in an attitude of soldier-like bolt-uprightness".

"In many cases, or even most, it will be best to have no border at all, but to make a slight preparation at the wall foot not apparently distinguishable from the path itself, and to have only an occasional plant or group or tuft of fern. Seeds will fall to this point, and the trailing and sheeting plants will clothe the wall foot and path edge, and the whole thing will look much better than if it had a stiffly edged border".

pleasanter than all the various ways of terraced treatment that may be practised with the help of dry-walling, that is to say, rough wall-building without mortar, especially where a suitable kind of stone can be had locally.

*   *   *

I doubt if there is any way in which a good quantity of plants, and of bushes of moderate size, can be so well seen and enjoyed as in one of these roughly terraced gardens, for one sees them up and down and in all sorts of ways, and one has a chance of seeing many lovely flowers clear against the sky, and of perhaps catching some sweetly-scented tiny thing like dianthus fragrans at exactly nose-height and eye-level, and so of enjoying its tender beauty and powerful fragrance in a way that had never before been found possible.

*   *   *

In place of all this easily attained prettiness how many gardens on sloping ground are disfigured by profitless and quite indefensible steep banks of mown grass! Hardly anything can be so undesirable in a garden. Such banks are unbeautiful, troublesome to mow, and wasteful of spaces that might be full of interest. If there must be a sloping space, and if for any reason there cannot be a dry wall, it is better to plant the slope with low bushy or rambling things; with creeping cotoneaster or Japan honeysuckle, with ivies, or with such bushes as savin, pyrus japonica, cistus, or berberis; or if it is on a large scale, with the free-growing rambling roses and double-flowered brambles. I name these things in preference to the rather over-done periwinkle and St. John's wort, because periwinkle is troublesome to weed, and soon grows into undesirably tight masses, and the hypericum, though sometimes of good effect, is extremely monotonous in large masses by itself, and is so ground-greedy that it allows of no companionship.

There is another great advantage to be gained by the use of the terrace walls; this is the display of the many shrubs as well as plants that will hang over and throw their flowering sprays all over the face of the wall.

In arranging such gardens, I like to have only a very narrow border at the foot of each wall, to accommodate such plants as the dwarf lavender . . . or any plant that is thankful for warmth or shelter.

*   *   *

"Many more beautiful garden-pictures may be made by variety in planting even quite straightly terraced spaces than at first appears possible, and the frequent flights of steps, always beautiful if easy and well proportioned, will be of the greatest value".
Beatrice Parsons, "Irises, Sedgwick Park".

"The hanging plants ... rock pinks and the like, though they grow quite happily on the level, do not show their true habit as they do when they are given the nearly upright wall out of which they can hang".

Many of the most easily grown alpines are just as happy in a sunny wall as in the shade. So beneficial to the root is contact with the cool stone, that plants that would perish from drought in the lighter soils and fierce sun-heat of our southern counties remain fresh and well nourished in a rock-wall in the hottest exposure. Moreover, in walls all plants seem to be longer lived. Those of the truly saxatile plants, whose way of growth is to droop over rocks and spread out flowering sheets, are never so happy as in a rock-wall ... In many of those rock-plants that are grown from seed, individuals will be found to vary, not only in the colour and size of the bloom, but in other characters, so that the plant cannot be judged by one example only.

* * *

Nothing is a better lesson in the knowledge of plants than to sit down in front of them, and handle them and look them over just as carefully as possible; and in no way can such study be more pleasantly or conveniently carried on than by taking a light seat to the rock-wall and giving plenty of time to each kind of little plant, examining it closely and asking oneself, and it, why this and why that? Especially if the first glance shows two tufts, one with a better appearance than the other; not to stir from the place until one has found out why and how it is done, and all about it. Of course a friend who has already gone through it all can help on the lesson more quickly, but I doubt whether it is not best to do it all for oneself.

* * *

When a wall garden has been established for some years one may expect all kinds of delightful surprises, for wind-blown seeds will settle in the joints and there will spring up thriving tufts of many a garden plant, perhaps of the most unlikely kind. Foxgloves, plants that in one's mind are associated with cool, woody hollows, may suddenly appear in a sunny wall, so may also the great garden mulleins. When this happens, and the roots travel back and find the coolness of the stone, the plants show astonishing vigour.

* * *

There is many a dismal wall, or court with paving right up to the wall, where the clever placing of some suitable plant in a chink of broken-cornered flag-stone, or empty joint close to the wall-foot, may redeem the dullness and want of interest of such a region of unbroken masonry. The plants most suitable for such a place are male fern and harts-tongue, Welsh poppy, and iris fœtidissima; all but the poppy having also the advantage of winter beauty. Just lately in my own home I have had an example of the willingness of a pretty plant to grow in the little space offered by the meeting of two paving-stones, one of which had lost an angle. Here a seed of mimulus cupreus grew self-sown, and the neat little plant, with its rich, deep orange bloom flowering all the summer, is a joy to see. This would also be a plant for the stone-paved sunless court with others of its family, including the common musk.

Woods and wild gardening

I am surprised to see the number and wonderful variety of the pictures of sylvan beauty that the wood displays throughout the year. I did not specially aim at variety, but, guided by the natural conditions of each region, tried to think out how best they might be fostered and perhaps a little bettered.

The only way in which variety of aspect was deliberately chosen was in the way of thinning out the natural growths. It was a wood of seedling trees ... and it seemed well to clear away all but one, or in some cases two kinds of trees in the several regions. Even in this the intention was to secure simplicity rather than variety, so that in moving about the ground there should be one thing at a time to see and enjoy... But it was done with the most careful watching, for there were to be no harsh frontiers. One kind of tree was to join hands with the next.

*   *   *

An unmade woodland track is the nearest thing to a road-poem that anything of the kind can show. It is full of a sympathetic mystery that inclines the mind to open wide in readiness to receive any impression that may be presented. The trees meet overhead; the light coming through the thick leafage is dim and green; the drowsy hum of many little winged creatures comes faintly from far overhead; the track winds, and one cannot see far onward. What will the next reach disclose? Some living wild thing, scarcely fearful because the way is so seldom used — squirrel, rabbit, red-deer, wild-boar? charcoal-burners, coming from the yet wilder wooded heights beyond? a knight in shining armour? a ring of fairies dancing under an oak? all equally possible in the dim green forest light.

And most mysterious of all are the tracks that pass through the woods of tall pines, for these woods are so solemn and so silent. Sometimes one may hear the harsh scream of the jay or the noisy flight of the wood-pigeon, but for the most part in windless weather they are almost without sound, for here there are none of the small song-birds that love the summer-leafing trees. Winter and summer these woods wear nearly the same aspect, except that the bracken that grows where the firs are thinnest, is green in summer and rusty-brown in winter. But where the trees stand thickly nothing grows upon the ground. Even moss is absent. The peaty earth shows purplish-grey through the dull brown of the carpet of fir-needle; the same colouring being exactly repeated in the trunks of the trees. The whole scene is painted in a monotone of purple-grey — solemn, quiet, by no means unbeautiful. And in harmony with the subdued colouring is the endless repetition of upright tree-stem, adding, as such an arrangement of line always does, to the impression of solemn dignity.

*   *   *

"Five woodland walks pass upward through the trees; every one has its own character, while the details change during its progress ... as if inviting the quiet stroller to stop a moment to enjoy some little woodland suavity".

But it is in the earlier summer that the shady depths will be fullest of beauty and interest. A fine lesson and example is a wood of wild bluebells in May; it shows the value of doing one thing at a time, and doing it largely and thoroughly well. But though planted wood gardens cannot give the space for such great shows as we see in the wild, yet they remind us of the use in shade of their near relations the Spanish squills (scilla campanulata), much like our bluebells in general appearance, and well adapted for planting in some quantity in shady places.

*　　*　　*

Some of the lilies are of wonderful beauty in the woodland. In no other garden use are they seen to such advantage, for they seem to give of their best when they are given a place where there is a surrounding of quiet conditions, and in some cases of isolation. Such a setting seems to be specially sympathetic to the stately lilium giganteum. It is at its best in thin woodland in a naturally rich soil... The fragrance is powerful and delicious, and carries far in the still summer evenings when the light is waning, at which time these grand lilies look their best.

*　　*　　*

One of the most precious things for careful planting, where the ground is cool and the shade is not too deep, but is such as will give a good background, is the lovely blue poppy meconopsis betonicifolia Baileyi. But, like many other good things, it should not be overdone. Twenty plants, in their groups of four or five, with single ones between, will make a better show than a hundred huddled together... This wonderful poppy varies in colour from a nearly pure blue, in shades both light and dark, to lilac or purplish tints. It is best to sacrifice these, pulling them up as soon as the colour of the bloom shows and carefully marking some of the best blues. Such care will be amply repaid by the improved colouring of the strain.

*　　*　　*

"Garland rose, where garden joins wood... The planting of hardy ferns should be one of the most beautiful forms of wild gardening. Though they are well suited for many uses in the garden proper, yet for their full enjoyment in fair quantity, the sentiment of association with shade in woody places is the one that is most sympathetic. Therefore a copse, or any kind of woodland that adjoins or approaches garden ground, should form the most desirable setting for the fern garden".

"Wild gardening is a delightful, and in good hands a most desirable, pursuit, but no kind of gardening is so difficult to do well, or is so full of pitfalls and of paths of peril".

Trees and honeysuckle

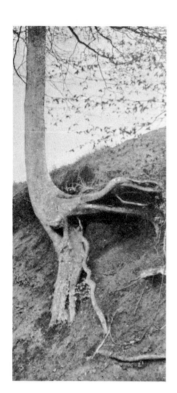

"The beech is evidently a tree with a strong instinct of self-preservation and no small degree of constructive ability".

Within half a mile of my home is a deep hollow lane whose steep sides are barred with strata of ragged sandstone, with layers of yellow sand between. In summer it is shaded by the wide-spreading branches of the trees, mostly beeches, that grow above. Some of these come forward to the actual edge of the scarp, and as there is no stone quite near the surface, the gradual crumbling away of the sandy earth where they first took root, threatens to leave the trees without support. Now the beech is evidently a tree with a strong instinct of self-preservation and no small degree of constructive ability, for I see that wherever this has happened the tree has thrown down a great stem-like root, a reversed counterpart of the stem above the ground level, that not only carries the weight with absolute security, but so well satisfies the eye of the critical observer that the tree looks as if it had support and to spare, and bears itself gracefully upon its admirably designed pillar. The root-stem seems to become a piece of tree trunk, and is covered with exactly the same kind of smooth bark as above ground. Several fair-sized beeches with trunks about from two and a half to three feet in diameter, have done the same thing, and in each case the sense of balance and adequate support could not have been better expressed.

One small beech with a trunk only as yet eight inches in diameter has one large backward root firmly clutching the bank... The little tree seems to have a perfect feeling for balance and construction, and its gracefully poised trunk shoots upward with a staunch consciousness of structural stability.

*   *   *

Many and various are the ways of the wild honeysuckle. In woody places it will trail about the ground and weave a loose copse-carpet from ankle to mid-leg deep, making many a snare for the unwary walker. One must step high and clear the foot each time, or one is likely to be thrown down by the tangled web of vegetable cordage. In this state it does not flower, but where there is a clearing and more light it takes advantage of any suitable support, and then seems to go up with a rush, and tumbles out in swags and garlands that in the long summer days are lovely and fragrant with the wealth of sweetly-scented bloom. During my wood walk I come upon a young oak with a trunk about a foot thick. I should judge that it is sixty feet high, and the top is full of honeysuckle. In this case the honeysuckle throws up three main stems from the ground. At a foot from the root two of these have twined together and make a fairly even two-stranded rope. A little higher they are joined by the third, and at six feet from the ground the three twine tightly and look like a badly-spun rope nearly two inches thick. So they advance up the tree, sometimes leaping away from each other and then again coming together and twining rope-fashion. The lowest branch of the oak must be twelve feet from the ground, and I do not know how the climber may have reached it, for it has only twined upon itself, not upon the tree, but there may have been smaller branches, since dead and fallen, that helped it to rise...

Smaller trees often suffer a good deal from the close constriction of the woody creeper. For the honeysuckle is a true tree, and its long stems are of true wood, of a quality both hard and tough, and all the tougher because the fibres of the individual stems are twisted like a rope... One young beech, whose stem is only four inches through, has thrown out thick swellings that look like a couple of close coils of a great python, and that more than double its diameter at the point of injury. The living honeysuckle is no longer there, but I suspect that some of its hard wood is enclosed within the swollen twists, and that throughout its lifetime the tree will bear the mark of the early injury.

Within a few paces a young oak, with a trunk five inches thick, is tightly girthed with close coils of honeysuckle. Some of the coils are deeply imbedded in the bark. This tree has also thrown out python-like swellings, which seem to close over and compress and strive to choke the invading climber. In some cases the grip is deadly to the honeysuckle; in others it still lives, buried in the substance of the oak. But if here and there it is gripped to death it matters little to the woodbine, whose assault is in force of numbers, for besides nine distinct coils round this young tree, there are eighteen ropes and cords leaping into it from below; some of them direct from the ground, and some from a young Spanish chestnut whose root is only three feet from that of the oak. I see that the original stem of the chestnut stops short about four feet from the ground, above which is eighteen inches of dead and rotting snag. It looks as if the fight between tree and climber had here ended in the tree's defeat, and as if its top had died and fallen, bringing down the honeysuckle to share and endure the ruin it had planned and brought about.

But the chestnut is evidently a clever and even crafty little tree, for not only has it repaired its disaster by throwing out a lusty young upward growth to take the place of its fallen top, but at the point where this springs from the short original trunk it has placed a small lateral branch which leads away the honeysuckle right into the neighbouring oak.

I do not know what ethical standard may prevail among vegetation, but it looks like a mean action on the part of the chestnut: to decoy the enemy away from himself, and to deliver his near neighbour into the same enemy's hands. Or is it an example of heroic self-sacrifice on the part of the oak? Perhaps the oak said, "Neighbour, throw out a little branch and send me the enemy. I am doomed already; a little more can only bring the end somewhat sooner. You have made one brave fight already, and though scarred for life, will live and do well. When I die and fall, as I must within a very few years, our enemy, now held up by me to the sunlight and gaily flowering, will lie in a mangled heap on the floor of the wood, where, overshadowed by your spreading branches, he will never bloom again but must remain content with a lowlier way of life." The little oak seems to be vainly striving for its life; it was gripped while still young, and the greater part of it is killed already — slowly but surely throttled by the deadly coils; indeed it is now no longer an oak tree but a honeysuckle tree.

"One young beech, whose stem is only four inches through, has thrown out thick swellings that look like a couple of close coils of a great python".

The heath garden

As in any other special garden whose name indicates the kind of plants grown in it, the occupants of the heath garden need not be absolutely restricted to heaths. The name should stand for a place of heaths mainly, with other plants and shrubs of the same botanical order (ericaceæ). This includes some of the most valuable of our small shrubs, such as pernettya, ledum, gaultheria and the several allied species that in gardens are commonly known as andromeda; also kalmia, rhododendron, azalea, and arbutus... Two other important families of plants will also find a place there, namely, the brooms and the hardier of the cistus.

*   *   *

I should always plant heaths in the long drifts that seems to me by far the most natural and pictorial way of placing most plants in rather wild places, and I would have them so that very few kinds were in sight at the same time. And I would have plants of different sizes, and sometimes a space of bare earth where their seed might fall and grow.

*   *   *

"White Cornish heath ... in the long drifts that seems to me by far the most natural and pictorial way of placing most plants in rather wild places".

Close masses of the early blooming erica carnea ... will suitably lead to some breadths of the late-flowering Cornish heath (erica vagans) of the type colour, in which an indefinite kind of low-toned pink prevails. At one point a little stream of the white variety will come well, and, further back, another such stream or drift of the redder kind... The native, and commonest of all, e. vulgaris or calluna, might then follow, treated in much the same way, with a ground work of the type intergrouped with long-shaped wedges or drifts of a few of the best varieties. These range from an unusually tall white to a dwarf form looking almost like a closely tufted moss.

The summer-blooming heath ... the bell heather (erica tetralix) will be kept towards the front on account of its rather low growth... For my own part I should have the type, already variable in its shades of pale pink, with the white only, and none darker ... I would also keep the tint light because the foliage has a general greyness, a colouring that in a good mass will be of considerable pictorial value as a break after the greener-leaved kinds, and that will serve to enhance the effect of those of rich green leafage, such as the daboëcia, and others, which are to follow later.

*   *   *

The paths in the heath garden should be either of the natural sandy earth or a short turf of the grasses proper to the poorest soil... They are of fine wiry leaf, not bright green like lawn grasses, but of a low-toned colouring that accords well with everything and competes with no other quiet foliage. Whether the path is of these fine grasses or of sand, there should be an abundance of the sweet wild thyme, while the paler-leaved thymus lanuginosus may well carpet some of the smaller grey-leaved heaths.

*   *   *

Climbing plants

To what extent it is desirable to have climbing plants on house walls is a question that often arises. In the case of many houses, either of mean or of over-pretentious architecture, the more they are covered up the better; for if their designer has left a building that can only be considered to be in bad taste, it behoves the gardener to do what he can to give it decent clothing... But in the case of a good building, though a carefully and duly restrained planting of its walls may give it an added grace, great care should be taken that nothing essential be hidden. Many a noble building has been shamefully buried under ivy; moulded doors and windows have been reduced to dark holes... But there are some plants that are singularly sympathetic to good buildings. Many a fine house of the eighteenth century is well graced by the noble foliage of a properly placed magnolia, with its large lustrous leaves and ivory cups of bloom. And a wistaria judiciously placed, carefully trained and restricted to a few level lines, is often helpful, and very beautiful with its clear-cut foliage and drooping clusters of light purple bloom.

*   *   *

For my own part I like to give a house, whatever its size or style, some dominant note in wall-planting. In my own home ... the prevailing wall-growths are vines and figs in the south and west, and in a shady northward facing court between two projecting wings, clematis montana on the two cooler sides, and again a vine upon the other. At one angle on the warmer side of the house, where the height to the eaves is not great, China roses have been trained up, and rosemary, which clothes the whole foot of the wall, is here encouraged to rise with them. The colour of the China rose bloom and the dusky green of the rosemary are always to me one of the most charming

"Wistaria misplaced ... in the case of a good building, though a carefully and duly restrained planting of its walls may give it an added grace, great care should be taken that nothing essential be hidden".

"In my own home ... the prevailing wall-growths are vines and figs in the south and west..."

combinations... I remember a cottage that had a porch covered with the golden balls of kerria japonica, and China roses reaching up the greater part of the low walls of half timber and plastering; the pink roses seeming to ask one which of them were the loveliest in colour; whether it was those that came against the silver-grey of the old oak or those that rested on the warm-white plaster. It should be remembered that of all roses the pink China is the one that is more constantly in bloom than any other, for its first flowers are perfected before the end of May and in sheltered places the later ones last till Christmas.

The clematis montana in the court riots over the wall facing east and up over the edge of the roof. At least it appears to riot, but is really trained and regulated; the training favouring its natural way of throwing down streamers and garlands of its long bloom-laden cordage. At one point it runs through and over a guelder rose that is its only wall companion. Then it turns to the left and is trained in garlands along a moulded oak beam that forms the base of a timbered wall with plastered panels.

But this is only one way of using this lovely climbing plant. Placed at the foot of any ragged tree — old worn-out apple or branching thorn — or a rough brake of bramble and other wild bushes, it will soon fill or cover it with its graceful growth and bounteous bloom. It will rush up a tall holly or clothe an old hedgerow where thorns have run up and become thin and gappy, or cover any unsightly sheds or any kind of outbuilding. All clematises prefer a chalky soil, but montana does not insist on this... In the end of May it comes into bloom, and is at its best in the early days of June. When the flowers are going over and the white petals show that slightly shrivelled surface that comes before they fall, they give off a sweet scent like vanilla. This cannot always be smelt from the actual flowers, but is carried by the air blowing over the flowering mass; it is a thing that is often a puzzle to owners of gardens some time in the second week of June.

"One cannot attempt to describe in detail all the beautiful ways of using such good things as clematis ... the tender grace of the best of the small white-bloomed clematis is never seen to better advantage than when wreathing and decorating".

"Clematis montana ... eager to rush up to a considerable height and then to tumble over with sheets of graceful foliage and cataracts of pure white bloom".

Another of these clematises, which, like the montana of gardens, is very near the wild species and is good for all the same purposes, is c. flammula, blooming in September. Very slightly trained it takes the form of flowery clouds... But this clematis has many other uses, for bowers, arches and pergolas, as well as for many varied aspects of wild gardening.

*　　*　　*

June is the time of some of the best of the climbing plants and slightly tender shrubs that we have against walls and treat as climbers, such as solanum crispum and abutilon vitifolium ... solanum crispum is much to be recommended in our southern counties. It covers a good space of wall, and every year shoots up some feet above it; indeed it is such a lively grower that it has to endure a severe yearly pruning. Every season it is smothered with its pretty clusters of potato-shaped bloom of a good bluish-lilac colour ... But the best of all climbing or rambling plants, whether for wall or arbour or pergola, is undoubtedly the grape-vine... To have it in fullest beauty it must ramp at will, for it is only when the fast-growing branches are thrown out far and wide that it fairly displays its graceful vigour and the generous magnificence of its incomparable foliage.

Clematis flammula rambles widely among other growths... I do not think there is any incident in my garden that has been more favourably noticed than the happy growth of clematis flammula and spiræa Lindleyana ... for the clematis bloom has the warm white of foam, and the spiræa has ... a graceful fern-like form".

Children and gardens

It is not at all an uncommon thing to find children's gardens in some unattractive, out-of-the-way corner, or, most commonly of all, under or too near trees, whose roots invade the space and render it a place that would be difficult to make anything of, even for persons of long experience. It is neither fair nor reasonable to give a child who wishes for a garden a place that is full of difficulties. I even think it is better that the children should not have to make their gardens at all from the beginning, unless any enterprising individual wishes to do so.

*　　*　　*

The late summer or early autumn is the time to begin the little gardens. The ground should be got ready not later than September, so that it will have time to settle before it is planted. Every detail should be exactly thought out beforehand, in order that, by the end of October or beginning of November, the plants may be put in their places. The children can be learning all the time. They should watch the whole operation and ask questions, and be told why everything is done.

Then, when in early spring the tips of the plants are pushing above ground and the snowdrops are showing their little white buds, the year's work will be beginning. The experienced elder should keep a close watch on the little gardens and their owners, and, week by week, should teach and show what is to be done. Weeding will be the first thing, and the little trugs will come out and the blunt weeding-knives to save fingers, and so on throughout the year.

* * *

"The daily tending of an already made garden is better to begin with; it is more interesting and inspiring, and the needs of the flowers can be seen and attended to with immediate result".

'Pricking off seedlings . . . the gardener will show you how to do it . . . and when you get handy I dare say he will be glad of your help".

If you lie on a table on your stomach and look over the edge, and if exactly below your eyes there is a dinner-plate on the floor, you see the plate in *plan*. But when a house is to be built or a garden is to be planned on uneven ground, you must also have a *section*... It supposes a cut straight through the ground. It is very seldom that such a cut is actually made, but it is a convenient way of showing levels... Then there is another point of view that is shown in drawings of buildings and in some ground-work. This is called the *elevation*. It is the view of anything upright, like any side of a house when you stand and look straight at it.

* * *

So to set out anything that is to be built, or ground-work that is to be shaped, you must have Plan, Section and Elevation ... If you put a cake on the floor and look at it from above, so that you see all the top and none of the sides, you will see it in *plan;* if you stand it up on anything about the level of your eye, you see it in *elevation;* if you cut it in half, each cut surface shows a *section*.

"Some common things shown in elevation, section and plan".

Sounds, sights and scents

Throughout my life I have found that one of the things most worth doing was to cultivate the habit of close observation... And I know from my own case that the will and the power to observe does not depend on the possession of keen sight. For I have sight that is both painful and inadequate... As if by way of compensation I have very keen hearing, and when I hear a little rustling rush in the grass and heath, or in the dead leaves under the trees, I can tell whether it is snake or lizard, mouse or bird. Many birds I am aware of only by the sound of their flight. I can nearly always tell what trees I am near by the sound of the wind in their leaves, though in the same tree it differs much from spring to autumn, as the leaves become of a harder and drier texture. The birches have a small, quick, high-pitched sound; so like that of falling rain that I am often deceived into thinking it really is rain, when it is only their own leaves hitting each other with a small rain-like patter. The voice of oak leaves is also rather high-pitched, though lower than that of birch. Chestnut leaves in a mild breeze sound much more deliberate; a sort of slow slither. Nearly all trees in gentle wind have a pleasant sound, but I confess to a distinct dislike of the noise of all the poplars; feeling it to be painfully fussy, unrestful, and disturbing. On the other hand, how soothing and delightful is the murmur of Scotch firs both near and far.

*   *   *

As for the matter of colour, what may be observed is simply without end. Those who have had no training in the way to see colour nearly always deceive themselves into thinking that they see it as they know it is locally, whereas the trained eye sees colour in due relation and as it truly *appears to be*. I remember driving with a friend of more than ordinary intelligence, who stoutly maintained that he saw the distant wooded hill quite as green as the near hedge. He knew it was green and could not see it otherwise, till I stopped at a place where a part of the face, but none of the sky-bounded edge of the wooded distance, showed through a tiny opening among the near green branches, when, to his immense surprise, he saw it was blue. A good way of showing the same thing is to tear a roundish hole in any large bright-green leaf such as a burdock, and to hold it at half-arm's length so that a part of a distant landscape is seen through the hole, and the eye sees also the whole surface of the leaf. As long as the sight takes in both, it will see the true relative colour of the distance.

*   *   *

On some of those cold, cloudless days of March, when the sky is of a darker and more intensely blue colour than one may see at any other time of the year, and geese are grazing on the wide strips of green common, so frequent in my neighbourhood, I have often noticed how surprisingly blue is the north side of a white goose. If at three o'clock in the afternoon of such a day one stands facing north-west and also facing the goose, its side next one's right hand is bright blue and its other side is bright yellow, deepening to orange as the sun "westers" and sinks.

"It always seems to me that one of the things most worth
doing about a garden is to try to make every part of it
beautiful... The gourd tribe alone will make a summer forest
of great leaf and even greater fruit..."

"... I have grown them of more than a hundred pounds
weight; this was over the low-tiled roof of some garden sheds.
The ordinary tiles were unable to bear the weight, so they
were replaced with a very large and strong tile, and each great
fruit as it grew was provided with blocks to keep it in place".

No year passes that one does not observe some charming combination of plants that one had not intentionally put together. Even though I am always trying to think of some such happy mixtures, others come of themselves. This year the best of these chances was a group of pale sulphur hollyhock seen against yews that were garlanded with clematis flammula; tender yellow and yellow-white and deepest green; upright spire of hollyhock, cloud-like mass of clematis, low-toned sombre ground of solemn yew... Others that I always delight in are of rosemary and China rose, and of China rose and tree ivy; of Jerusalem sage (phlomis) and mullein (verbascum phlomoides); of London pride and St. Bruno's lily; of gypsophila and globe thistle; of dark-flowered honesty and the large, handsome variety of megasea cordifolia. Then there are the many associations of bluish and grey-leaved plants, as of lyme grass and lavender cotton and catmint, and these also with lavender and its dwarf dark variety and the pretty sisyrinchium Bermudiana.

"Lyme grass and lavender cotton... No year passes that one does not observe some charming combination of plants".

*   *   *

There is a class of scent that, though it can neither be called sweet nor aromatic, is decidedly pleasing and interesting. Such is that of bracken and other fern-fronds, ivy-leaves, box-bushes, vine-blossom, elderflowers and fig-leaves. There are the sweet scents that are wholly delightful — most of the roses, honeysuckle, primrose, cowslip, mignonette, pink, carnation, helio-trope, lily of the valley, and a host of others; then there is a class of scent that is intensely powerful, and gives an impression almost of intemperance or voluptuousness, such as magnolia, tuberose, gardenia, stephanotis, and jasmine; it is strange that these all have white flowers of thick leathery texture. In strongest contrast to these are the sweet, wholesome, wind-wafted scents of clover-field, of bean-field, and of new-mown hay, and the soft honey-scent of sun-baked heather, and of a buttercup meadow in April. Still more delicious is the wind-swept sweetness of a wood of larch or of Scotch fir, and the delicate perfume of young-leaved birch, or the heavier scent of the flowering lime. Out on the moorlands, besides the sweet heather-scent, is that of flowering broom and gorse and of the bracken, so like the first smell of the sea as you come near it after a long absence.

*   *   *

Perhaps the most delightful of all flower scents are those whose tender and delicate quality makes one wish for just a little more. Such a scent is that of apple-blossom, and of some small pansies, and of the wild rose and the honeysuckle. Among roses alone the variety and degree of sweet scent seems almost infinite. To me the sweetest of all is the Provence, the old cabbage rose of our gardens. When something approaching this appears, as it frequently does, among the hybrid perpetuals, I always greet it as the real sweet rose smell.

*   *   *

I observe that when a rose exists in both single and double form the scent is increased in the double beyond the proportion that one would expect. Rosa lucida in the ordinary single state has only a very slight scent; in the lovely double form it is very sweet, and has acquired somewhat of the moss-rose smell.

* * *

Sometimes I have met with a scent of ... mysterious and aromatic kind when passing near a bank clothed with the great St. John's wort. As this occurs in early autumn, I suppose it to be occasioned by the decay of some of the leaves. And there is a small yellow-flowered potentilla that has a scent of the same character, but always freely and willingly given off — a humble-looking little plant, well worth growing for its sweetness.

* * *

"Rose petals for pot-pourri... The roses must be in good order. They may be full blown, but must not be faded or in any way injured, and above all they must be quite dry. A rose is a great hand at holding water".

Among the many wonders of the vegetable world are the flowers that hang their heads and seem to sleep in the daytime, and that awaken as the sun goes down, and live their waking life at night... It is vain to try and smell the night-given scent in the daytime; it is either withheld altogether, or some other smell, quite different, and not always pleasant, is there instead... the finest fragrance comes from the small annual night-scented stock (matthiola bicornis), a plant that in daytime is almost ugly; for the leaves are of a dull-grey colour, and the flowers are small and also dull-coloured, and they are closed and droop and look unhappy. But when the sun has set the modest little plant seems to come to life; the grey foliage is almost beautiful in its harmonious relation to the half-light; the flowers stand up and expand, and in the early twilight show tender colouring of faint pink and lilac, and pour out upon the still night-air a lavish gift of sweetest fragrance.

* * *

But of all the sweet scents of bush or flower, the ones that give me the greatest pleasure are those of the aromatic class, where they seem to have a wholesome resinous or balsamic base, with a delicate perfume added. When I pick and crush in my hand a twig of bay, or brush against a bush of rosemary, or tread upon a tuft of thyme, or pass through incense-laden brakes of cistus, I feel that here is all that is best and purest and most refined, and nearest to poetry, in the range of faculty of the sense of smell.

Weeds and pests

Weeding is a delightful occupation, especially after summer rain, when the roots come up clear and clean. One gets to know how many and various are the ways of weeds — as many almost as the moods of human creatures. How easy and pleasant to pull up are the soft annuals like chickweed and groundsel, and how one looks with respect at deep-rooted things like docks, that make one go and fetch a spade. Comfrey is another thing with a terrible root, and every bit must be got out, as it will grow again from the smallest scrap.

* * *

Of bird, beast, and insect pests we have plenty. First, and worst, are rabbits. They will gnaw and nibble anything and everything that is newly planted... The necessity of wiring everything newly planted adds greatly to the labour and expense of the garden, and the unsightly grey wire-netting is an unpleasant eyesore. When plants or bushes are well established the rabbits leave them alone, though some families of plants are always irresistible — pinks and carnations, for instance, and nearly all cruciferæ, such as wallflowers, stocks and iberis. The only plants I know that they do not touch are rhododendrons and azaleas; they leave them for the hare, that is sure to get in every now and then, and who stands up on his long hind-legs, and will eat rose-bushes quite high up.

Plants eaten by a hare look as if they had been cut with a sharp knife; there is no appearance of gnawing or nibbling, no ragged edges of wood or frayed bark, but just a straight clean cut.

Field mice are very troublesome. Some years they will nibble off the flower-buds of the Lent hellebores; when they do this they have a curious way of collecting them and laying them in heaps. I have no idea why they do this, as they neither carry them away nor eat them afterwards; there the heaps of buds lie till they rot or dry up. They once stole all my auricula seed in the same way. I had marked some good plants for seed, cutting off all the other flowers as soon as they went out of bloom. The seed was ripening, and I watched it daily, awaiting the moment for harvesting. But a few days before it was ready I went round and found the seed was all gone; it had been cut off at the top of the stalk, so that the umbel-shaped heads had been taken away whole. I looked about, and luckily found three slightly hollow places under

"In the big weeding basket... Weeding is a delightful occupation, especially after summer rain, when the roots come up clear and clean".

the bank at the back of the border where the seed-heads had been piled in heaps. In this case it looked as if it had been stored for food; luckily it was near enough to ripeness for me to save my crop.

*　　*　　*

Pheasants are very bad gardeners; what they seem to enjoy most are crocuses — in fact, it is no use planting them. I had once a nice collection of crocus species... One day when I came to see my crocuses, I found where each patch had been a basin-shaped excavation and a few fragments of stalk or some part of the plant. They had begun at one end and worked steadily along, clearing them right out.

But we have one grand consolation in having no slugs, at least hardly any that are truly indigenous; they do not like our dry, sandy heaths. Friends are very generous in sending them with plants, so that we have a moderate number that hang about frames and pot plants, though nothing much to boast of; but they never trouble seedlings in the open ground, and for this I can never be too thankful.

The kitchen garden

Much as I love the flower garden and the woodland, I am by no means indifferent to the interest and charm of the kitchen garden. For though its products are for the most part utilitarian, they all have their life-histories, and on the rare occasions when I am free to take a quiet stroll for pure pleasure of the garden I often take it among the vegetables. I cannot help thinking of what immense importance in our life and health and well-being are the patiently gained developments of even one alone of the many families of kitchen-garden plants. When I have seen in rocky places on our English and other coasts, a straggling plant with broad glaucous leaves, I have always looked upon it with sincere respect; for this wild plant is the parent of all the members of the great cabbage tribe. And then I think of the many hundreds of years that it has been patiently cultivated, until little by little it has been driven by careful selection and keen observation into the many forms it now takes in our gardens and on our tables. For not only do the different shapes of cabbage, of all sorts and sizes — round, flattened, or pointed — of loose, open shape like a rose, or tight and hard as a drumhead — come from this one wild plant, but also the many varieties of cauliflower and broccoli, where the parts most developed are the flower-bud and thickened flower-stalk. And besides these there are the kinds selected for their hardiness, and by slow degrees coaxed and persuaded into taking the forms of the winter kales, some nearly smooth of leaf, but often with the leaf-edges heavily curled. Then another of the hardiest of these winter green things is the Brussels sprout, its stem thickly set with tiny little tight cabbages just the size for a doll's dinner-table

*　　*　　*

All gardeners know that radishes should be grown as quickly as possible; a slow-grown radish is like slowly-made toast, hard and tough and distasteful.

"On the rare occasions when I am free to take a quiet stroll for pure pleasure of the garden I often take it among the vegetables".
T. Knox, "Cottage garden".

A learned garden-friend once said to me, "Grow your radishes in nearly pure leaf-mould". I tried growing them in well-decayed leaf-mould without admixture in late summer in a half-shaded place, and kept them well watered; and though the leaves were a little drawn, never did I eat such radishes for delicate, crisp, wet tenderness.

*   *   *

I wish all growing things were as clearly and distinctively named as the broad bean; for I know no plant that in nearly all its parts and phases and aspects displays so visibly the quality of breadth. What pair of seed-leaves are so absurdly broad? and how broad is the leaf and the pod and the bean within, and how thick the stem! But as if to redeem the broad bean from a certain stiffness and want of grace shown by the whole plant, there is the pretty flower of white and black; the white of the soft quality that is seen in white velvet, and the black the richest of brown-blacks, also of a velvety texture.

*   *   *

The first tender little green peas, how delicious they are; their delicate sweetness makes them almost more like some dainty fruit than a serious food-stuff such as comes under the rude general classification of "green vegetables"; and how good are the first dwarf French beans, and what a staunch friend of late summer and autumn is the trusty scarlet runner.

*   *   *

A good crop of onions is a joy to the culinary corner of the gardener's heart, and I always think there is something highly pictorial about the great silvery seed-heads of the few we keep for seed, borne high on the tall flower-stalk with its curious swollen base. Shallots stand like soldiers in their ranks, so neatly and evenly do they grow, with their dark-green upright leaves looking like well-to-do patches of jonquil. Chives is a neat edging-plant, growing in close tufts, the chopped leaves good in salads. A row of leeks is a pleasant sight, both growing and served in a dish as a green vegetable; the mildest of all the onion tribe.

*   *   *

One other department of the garden is a source of pleasure, namely, a border or little garden for the sweet-herbs. Where house and garden are newly made I like to arrange places for these herbs not in the kitchen garden only, but that there should be also close to the house, and somewhere near the door that gives access to the kitchen, a little herb-garden for the cook, so that any herb can be had at once. Here should be two or three plants each of the thymes, basils, and savouries, tarragon and chervil, a bush of sage, some clumps of balm, marjoram, and fennel, soup-celery and parsley for flavouring, borage and a little mint, and within reach a bay-tree.

Cut flowers

One can hardly go wrong if a bunch of any one kind of flower is cut with long stalks and plenty of its own leafage, and especially if it is cut without

"Canterbury bells... I cannot explain why it is, but have always observed that no intentional arrangement of flowers in the ordinary way gives an effect so good as that of a bunch held easily in the hand as flower by flower is cut, and put in water without fresh arrangement".

66

carrying a basket. I cannot explain why it is, but have always observed that no intentional arrangement of flowers in the ordinary way gives an effect so good as that of a bunch held easily in the hand as flower by flower is cut, and put in water without fresh arrangement. The only glimmer of a reason I can see for it is that they are cut of uneven lengths, and that the natural way of carrying them in the hands is with the stalks fairly even, and that this gives just that freedom of top outline that is so much to be desired.

*   *   *

Though glass things are in many ways the pleasantest and prettiest and cleanest to put our home flowers in, and though there is a certain satisfaction in seeing the stalks, and knowing that we can all the more readily come to the rescue by seeing the water becoming foul or low, yet in almost every house there are cherished flower-holders of other material than glass. Among those I have in constant use are bowls and jars of the ever-beautiful porcelains of China and Japan, English makes of Worcester and of the delicate cream-white earthenware of Wedgwood, old Italian majolica, glazed pottery from all Europe and some of Asia and Africa, Indian brass lotahs and large Dutch and Venetian pails and jugs and wine-coolers of beaten copper. Some of the latter are more generally used for pot-plants, but when flowers are large and in plenty, as at the times of tulip and rhododendron and paeony, the most roomy things one has are none too large.

As in all matters of decoration, so also it should be borne in mind in the use of flowers indoors that one of the first and wholesomest laws is that of restraint and moderation. So great is the love of flowers nowadays, and so mischievous is the teaching of that hackneyed saying which holds that "you cannot have too much of a good thing", that people often fall into the error of having much too much of flowers and foliage in their rooms. There comes a point where the room becomes overloaded with flowers and greenery. During the last few years I have seen many a drawing-room where it appeared to be less a room than a thicket.

Left, "Rose Gloire Lyonnaise... As in all matters of decoration, so also it should be borne in mind in the use of flowers indoors that one of the first and wholesomest laws is that of restraint and moderation".

Above, "Midsummer paeonies ... when flowers are large and in plenty ... the most roomy things one has are none too large".

"A few years ago, as it was impossible to find any kind of basket that was satisfactory, especially for flowers cut with long stems, I took some pains to design one".

"I observe that when a rose exists in both single and double form the scent is increased in the double beyond the proportion that one would expect".
George S. Elgood, "Viscountess Folkestone".

"My orchard garden would run into a good many acres, but every year it would be growing into beauty and profit. The grass should be left rough, and plentifully planted with daffodils, and with cowslips if the soil is strong. The grass would be mown and made into hay in June, and perhaps mown once more towards the end of September. Under the ... trees would be primroses and the garden kinds of wood hyacinths and dog-tooth violets and lily of the valley, and perhaps snowdrops, or any of the smaller bulbs that most commended themselves to the taste of the master".
A.A. Glendening, "Picking flowers".

People and practices

I shall never forget a visit to a nursery some six-and-twenty years ago. It was walled all round, and a deep-sounding bell had to be rung many times before any one came to open the gate; but at last it was opened by a fine, strongly-built, sunburnt woman of the type of the good working farmer's wife, that I remember as a child... One of the specialties of the place was a fine breed of mastiffs; another was an old black Hamburg vine, that rambled and clambered in and out of some very old greenhouses, and was wonderfully productive. There were alleys of nuts in all directions, and large spreading patches of palest yellow daffodils — the double narcissus cernuus, now so scarce and difficult to grow. Had I then known how precious a thing was there in fair abundance, I should not have been contented with the modest dozen that I asked for. It was a most pleasant garden to wander in, especially with the old Mr. Webb who presently appeared. He was dressed in black clothes of an old-looking cut — a Quaker, I believe. Never shall I forget an apple-tart he invited me to try as a proof of the merit of the "Wellington" apple. It was not only good, but beautiful; the cooked apple looking rosy and transparent, and most inviting. He told me he was an ardent preacher of total abstinence, and took me to a grassy, shady place among the nuts, where there was an upright stone slab, like a tombstone, with the inscription:

TO ALCOHOL

He had dug a grave, and poured into it a quantity of wine and beer and spirits, and placed the stone as a memorial of his abhorrence of drink. The whole thing remains in my mind like a picture — the shady groves of old nuts, in tenderest early leaf, the pale daffodils, the mighty chained mastiffs with bloodshot eyes and murderous fangs, the brawny, wholesome woman, and the trim old gentleman in black. It was the only nursery I ever saw where one would expect to see fairies on a summer night.

*   *   *

I knew an old labourer who died of a rose-prick. He used to work about the roads, and at cleaning the ditches and mending the hedges. For some time I did not see him and when I asked another old countryman, "What's gone o' Master Trussler?" the answer was, "He's dead — died of a canker-bush". The wild dog-rose is still the "canker" in the speech of the old people, and a thorn or prickle is still a "bush". A dog-rose prickle had gone deep into the old hedger's hand — a "bush" more or less was nothing to him, but the neglected little wound had become tainted with some impurity, blood-poisoning had set in, and my poor old friend had truly enough "died of a canker-bush".

*   *   *

Is it only an instance of patriotic prejudice, or is it really, as I believe, a fact, that no country roads and lanes in the temperate world are so full of sweet and homely pictorial incident as those of our dear England? For apart from the living pictures of tree and bush, fern and flower, rampant tangle and

"In the old cottages we find the true old country people ... who still retain the speech and ways of thought and plain simple dress of the early part of the century".

garland of wild rose and honeysuckle, hop and briony, and of all these combined with rocky bank and mossy slope, there are the many incidents of human interest... The comfortable farmstead, almost a village in itself, with its farmhouse and one or two cottages, its barns, stables, cowhouses and piggeries, waggon sheds and granaries. The cottages are of the older type, built before the times of easy communication, when what are now well-kept by-roads were only sandy tracks. They are precious examples of the true buildings of the country, for they must have been made of the material available from within a few miles only, and they were built by the men who knew no other ways of working than those of their fathers before them. This is why these farms and cottages seem to grow out of the ground.

*   *   *

It is in the old cottages that we find the true old country people, some of whose womenkind have hardly ever been more than ten miles from home; people who still retain the speech and ways of thought and plain simple dress of the early part of the century. All my life I can remember my old friend with the donkey-cart, in intimate association with the lanes near my home. He worked under the road-surveyor, trimming overgrowing hedges and road edges, and removing incidental obstructions, as of the many hazels pulled down and left hanging into the road by nut-hunting boys in September, and boughs blown down by winter storms, and drifts of dead leaves in November. The white donkey, who carried tools and worker, waited all day on some handy wayside patch of grass where he found food and rest. Man and beast grew old together in many a long year's companionship of toil, until at length neither could work any longer. A farmer who was a kind neighbour to the old man told me a pathetic story of how he had come to ask him to shoot the old donkey, who could no longer feed and was evidently very near his end. "The old man he sobbed and cried something turrible", said my friend the farmer. Afterwards, when I asked how old the donkey was, and how long the two had worked together, the old road-man said: "I know his age exactly; he is the same age as my youngest son, and that's twenty-seven."

*   *   *

"The comfortable farmstead, almost a village in itself, with its farmhouse and one or two cottages, its barns, stables, cowhouses and piggeries, waggon sheds and granaries".

"All my life I can remember my old friend with the donkey-cart... Man and beast grew old together in many a long year's companionship of toil, until at length neither could work any longer".

"The Hut... When on winter evenings there is a great log-fire blazing, and hot elder-wine is ready for drinking and nuts waiting to be cracked ... it is a very cosy and cheerful place".

While my larger cottage was building I lived in the tiny one just across the lawn that had been built a couple of years before [The Hut]... Before I had occasion to live there myself I had lent it to an old cottager friend, a woman of the true old country type now, alas, nearly extinct. In her day she had been a fine hard worker, but rheumatism and heart-trouble put a painful restriction on her ability to do the work that her brave old heart made her unwilling to give up. I had hoped when I wanted the cottage for my own use to be able to keep her there as my servant. Her beautiful cleanliness and ready cheerfulness, her bright, kindly, apple-cheeked face, her delicious old caps and plain dress of old-world pattern, were so exactly in keeping with the simple little cottage that I was unwilling to let her go, but after a few weeks it became clear that her strength was not equal to keeping the house for both of us, and as her knowledge of cooking was less than rudimentary, I had to find for her a home in the village and for myself a more able-bodied helper. Dear old soul, what delicious, inconsequent, good-natured gossip she used to pour forth; a little difficult to follow, because as a rule all nominatives were omitted; and as I could not by intuition keep up with the discursive workings of her brain, nor at once grasp the identity indicated by "she", with a fling of the head or jerk of the thumb towards some distant farm; and as the disjointed fragments of narrative ran into one another, or rather flowed out of one another in a constant flood of small digression, the end of the story left me much where I was at the beginning.

But I wish I could remember all the odd tricks of speech and local manner

"Ever since it came to me to feel some little grasp of knowledge of means and methods, I have found that my greatest pleasure ... has been in the enjoyment of beauty of a pictorial kind". Mildred Anne Butler, "Hollyhocks and poppies".

"Lady Coventry's needlework ... is a pretty Midland name for the good garden plant commonly called red valerian... How the name originated cannot be exactly stated ... it may be assumed that some Lady Coventry [of the late eighteenth century] was specially fond of the pretty needlecraft so widely practised among the ladies of that time... It is easy to see how the red valerian came to be used as a model for needlework. Short stitches and long would easily render the small divisions of the calyx and the long slender spur and single pistil, and a quantity of this, representing the rather crowded flower-head, would have a very good effect on a white or light ground.

"The plant itself is a pretty one in any garden. Botanists say that it is not indigenous, but it has taken to the country and acclimatised itself, and now behaves like a native... It is a capital plant for establishing on or in walls or bold rockwork, as well as in the garden border. It is always thankful for chalk or lime in any form".
George S. Elgood, "Lady Coventry's needlework".

"The lane of the ghost cart..."

of wording. There was one story of a woman who met a toad coming downstairs. The toad bit the woman in the arm — I could not bear to spoil the story by telling her that toads had no teeth: "And her arm got *that* bad — there — it *was* bad, that it was! She had to have it off, she did!" This wonderful story came up one day when I came in to tea and found a fine, handsome toad sitting on the raised brick hearth. It is strange how the country folk still believe in the venom of toads.

One day I found her groaning in the kitchen and asked what ailed her. "It's my rheumatics; they do crucify me that crool!" And then she told how she had often worked in the fields in wet weather, topping and tailing turnips and suchlike work, soaked through and through, and on one worst day of all in thin boots: "My thick ones was gone to be mended".

* * *

I was riding a big and rather nervous horse down a lane, which, though not exactly steep, has a fairly sharp fall. There had been a sudden and heavy storm of summer rain, and I had just ridden out from the shelter of a thickly-leafed oak, when I heard a two-wheeled country cart driving rather fast down the narrow lane behind me. As it came near, I judged by the sound that it was a heavy tax-cart such as a farmer would drive to market with two or three pigs behind him under a strong pig-net. I could hear the chink and rattle of the harness and of the loose ends of the tail-board chains. As the man driving was just about to pass me, he slapped the reins down on the horse's back, as a rough driver does who has no whip, and I noticed the sodden sound of the wet leather; at the same moment he gave a "dchk" to urge the horse. I was in the act of drawing my horse close to the near side of the lane, when, hearing the man, he made an impatient sort of bucking jump, followed by a moderate kick. The passing cart was so close that I thought his heels must touch the wheel, but they did not, and again I drew him as near as I could to the bank. As the cart did not pass I looked round, and as I turned the sound ceased, and nothing was to be seen but some hundred yards or so of the empty space of the hollow roadway.

* * *

The love of gardening has so greatly grown and spread within the last few years, that the need of really good and beautiful garden flowers is already far in advance of the demand for the so-called "florists" flowers, by which I mean those that find favour in the exclusive shows of societies for the growing and exhibition of such flowers as tulips, carnations, dahlias, and chrysanthemums... I am of opinion that the show-table is unworthily used when its object is to be an end in itself, and that it should be only a means to a better end, and that when it exhibits what has become merely a "fancy", it loses sight of its honourable position as a trustworthy exponent of horti-culture, and has degenerated to a baser use.

* * *

It is important to train oneself to have a good flower-eye; to be able to see at a glance what flowers are good and which are unworthy, and why, and to keep an open mind about it; not to be swayed by the petty tyrannies of the "florist" or show judge; for, though some part of his judgement may be sound, he is himself a slave to rules and must go by points which are defined arbitrarily and rigidly, and have reference mainly to the show-table, leaving out of account, as if unworthy of consideration, such matters as gardens and garden beauty, and human delight, and sunshine, and varying lights of morning and evening and noonday.

*   *   *

An artificial rockery is usually a bit of frankly simple make-believe... And even if for a moment one succeeds in cheating oneself into thinking that it is something like a bit of rocky nature, there is pretty sure to be the zinc label, with its stark figure and ghastly colouring, looking as if it were put there of cruel purpose for the more effectual shattering of the vain illusion. I suppose that of all metallic surfaces there is none so unlovely as that of zinc, and yet we stick upright strips of it among, and even in front of some of the daintiest of our tiny plants. We spend thought and money, and still more money's-worth in time and labour, on making our little rocky terraces, and perhaps succeed in getting them into nice lines and planted with the choicest things, and then we peg it all over with zinc labels! I am quite in sympathy with those who do not know their plants well enough to do without the labels; I have passed through that stage myself, and there are many cases where the label must be there. But I considered that in dressed ground or pure pleasure ground, where the object is some scheme of garden beauty, the label, even if it must be there, should never be seen. I felt this so keenly myself when I first had a piece of rock-garden that I hit upon a plan that can be confidently recommended: that of driving the ugly thing into the earth, leaving only just enough above ground to lay hold of... In my own later practice, where the number of different plants has been reduced to just those I like best and think most worthy of a place, they are so well known to me that their names are as familiar as those of my best friends; and when I admit a new plant, if I cannot at once learn its name, it is purposely given a big ugly label, as a self-inflicted penance that shall continue until such time as I can expiate by remembrance.

*   *   *

I was delighted [at a London nursery] to see the use as labels of old wheel-spokes. I could not help feeling that if one had been a spoke of a cab-wheel, and had passed all one's working life in being whirled and clattered over London pavements, defiled with street mud, how pleasant a way to end one's days was this; to have one's felloe end pointed and dipped in nice wholesome rot-resisting gas-tar and thrust into the quiet cool earth, and one's nave end smoothed and painted and inscribed with some such soothing legend as vinca minor or dianthus fragrans!

"It is amusing to dress up a snapdragon seed-pod, when it is brown and dry, as an old woman. If you look at it you will see how curiously like a face it is, with large eyes and open mouth. You must break off the projecting spike so that it leaves a little turned-up snub nose... Anyone who can dress dolls can make this. If you shake her she weeps little black tears".

"While May is still young . . . the grass grows tall and strong under the half shade of the old apple-trees, some of the later kinds being still loaded with bloom".
Beatrice Parsons, "Wild Gardens, St. Hilda's, Oxford".

Spring

A March study — Lent hellebores — The arrival of spring
Flowering bulbs — Violets — The spring garden — The copse in March and April
The scents of spring — The rock garden in April
Periwinkles and wallflowers — Tulips — Spring shrubs
A wood ramble in April — Wood plants — Grouping flowers — Rhododendrons
Queen wasps — Spring flowers for decoration — Spring wild flowers in the house

A March study

There comes a day towards the end of March when there is but little wind, and that is from the west or even south-west. The sun has gained much power, so that it is pleasant to sit out in the garden, or, better still, in some sunny nook of sheltered woodland. There is such a place among silver-trunked birches, with here and there the splendid richness of masses of dark holly. The rest of the background above eye-level is of the warm bud-colour of the summer-leafing trees, and, below, the fading rust of the now nearly flattened fronds of last year's bracken, and the still paler drifts of leaves from neighbouring oaks and chestnuts. The sunlight strikes brightly on the silver stems of the birches, and casts their shadows clear-cut across the grassy woodland ride. The grass is barely green as yet, but has the faint winter green

"A day comes ... when the wind, now breathing gently from the south-west, puts new life into all growing things".
W. Curtis, "Many-flowered narcissus", from The Botanical Magazine.

"Where [tracks] pass through the birch copse, the daffodils have been planted in the shallow hollows of the old ways".

of herbage not yet grown and still powdered with the short remnants of the fine-leaved, last-year-mown heath grasses. Brown leaves still hang on young beech and oak. The trunks of the Spanish chestnuts are elephant-grey, a notable contrast to the sudden, vivid shafts of the birches. Some groups of the pale early Pyrenean daffodil gleam level on the ground a little way forward.

It is the year's first complete picture of flower-effect in the woodland landscape.

* * *

There is a pleasant mass of colour showing in the wood-edge on the dead-leaf carpet. It is a straggling group of daphne mezereum, with some clumps of red Lent hellebores, and, to the front, some half-connected patches of the common dog-tooth violet. The nearly related combination of colour is a delight to the trained colour-eye. There is nothing brilliant; it is all restrained — refined; in harmony with the veiled light that reaches the flowers through the great clumps of hollies and tall half-overhead chestnuts and neighbouring beech. The colours are all a little "sad", as the old writers so aptly say of the flower-tints of secondary strength. But it is a perfect picture. One comes to it again and again as one does to any picture that is good to live with.

* * *

These early examples within the days of March are of special interest because as yet flowers are few; the mind is less distracted by much variety than later in the year, and is more readily concentrated on the few things that may be done and observed; so that the necessary restriction is a good preparation, by easy steps, for the wider field of observation that is presented later.

Now we pass on through the dark masses of rhododendron and the birches that shoot up among them. How the silver stems, blotched and banded with varied browns and greys so deep in tone that they show like a luminous black, tell among the glossy rhododendron green; and how strangely different is the way of growth of the two kinds of tree; the tall white trunks spearing up through the dense, dark, leathery leaf-masses of solid, roundish outline, with their delicate network of reddish branch and spray gently swaying far overhead!

Lent hellebores

The Lent hellebores are by no means so generally cultivated as their undoubted merit deserves, for at their time of blooming, from the end of February to nearly through March, they are the most important of the flowering plants of their season, both for size and general aspect. They are well suited to some place where wood and garden meet, and are also good at shrubbery edges, for they hold their foliage all the summer and are never unsightly. One would like to plant a whole garden of them in the nearer part of some wood where primroses and bluebells come naturally, in cool soil enriched with its own leaf mould, and to have them grouped with a following

"Lent hellebores in the nut walk... They are well suited to some place where wood and garden meet, and are also good at shrubbery edges, for they hold their foliage all the summer and are never unsightly".

of hardy ferns, sheltered by hazels and occasional oaks. In my own garden I have them in borders of a nut walk, a place that suits them well, for by the time the young foliage is growing the leaves are coming on the nuts and giving just the amount of shade that is most beneficial.

The arrival of spring

In the end of March, or at any time during the month when the wind is in the east or north-east, all increase and development of vegetation appears to cease. As things are, so they remain. Plants that are in flower retain their bloom, but, as it were, under protest. A kind of sullen dullness pervades all plant life. Sweet-scented shrubs do not give off their fragrance; even the woodland moss and earth and dead leaves withhold their sweet, nutty scent. The surface of the earth has an arid, infertile look; a slight haze of an ugly grey takes the colour out of objects in middle distance, and seems to rob the flowers of theirs, or to put them out of harmony with all things around. But a day comes, or, perhaps, a warmer night, when the wind, now breathing gently from the south-west, puts new life into all growing things. A marvellous change is wrought in a few hours. A little warm rain has fallen, and plants, invisible before, and doubtless still underground, spring into glad life.

Flowering bulbs

It will be the daffodils that come first to mind when it is a question of arranging and grouping hardy bulbous plants. For these there is no better place than a stretch of thin woodland, where they can be seen both far and near. For the manner of the planting, on which much of the success of the display depends, it may be confidently recommended that they should also be placed in long drifts, more or less parallel, and that these should also be more or less parallel with the path from which they will be seen. A pattern something like long-shaped fish is advised, all going in one direction in a thin, open shoal, and the actual bulbs clustered or scattered within the fish-like outline.

When ample space has to be dealt with, there may be three or four of these drifts of the same kind, and it is interesting and instructive, as well as good to see, to have the whole arrangement of kinds in a proper sequence as to species and hybrids.

"Where the wood is large and trees grow thinly it is a precious opportunity for planting daffodils in quantity".

*   *   *

Besides the daffodils, there are one or two classes of bulbs that are better suited for growing in quantity by themselves, than in lesser numbers in combination with other plants. Crocuses ... are seen at their best in a half-wild place, such as where garden gives place either to open or to thinly wooded parkland, and where they are beyond the influence of the mowing machine, for they need the full growth of the foliage that goes on after the bloom is over. Moreover, they are so bright and showy that they would outshine and

"It must have been at about seven years of age that I first learnt to know and love a primrose copse. Since then more than half a century has passed, and yet each spring, when I wander into the primrose wood, and see the pale yellow blooms, and smell their sweetest of sweet scents, and feel the warm spring air throbbing with the quickening pulse of new life, and hear the glad notes of the birds and the burden of the bees, and see again the same delicate young growths piercing the mossy woodland carpet; when I see and feel and hear all this, for a moment I am seven years old again and wandering in the fragrant wood.
Charles E. Wilson, "Gathering Primroses".

overpower others of the smaller bulbs that flower at the same time, and therefore, as a main rule, they are better kept apart.

In the cases of crocuses it is best that they should be planted in drifts of one kind, or at least of one colour at a time, and preferably in the way described for daffodils. Many a good place has been spoilt by an unwary planting of a quantity of cheap bulbs in mixture. Like all else in good gardening, there should be a definite intention towards some aspect of pictorial beauty. Thus the purple crocuses might come first, followed by, or at one end intergrouped with, the white. If crocus space is limited, the yellows could follow, but they would be better apart, in a generous planting by themselves.

The common snowdrops, in the heavy or chalky soils that they prefer, are also good in large sheets or groups by themselves. In such places they increase and spread and form such lovely pictures of plant beauty that one does not wish to add anything that would distract the attention from the one complete and simple effect. It should be remembered, in establishing a plantation of snowdrops, that they are thankful for deep planting.

"The snowdrop is, for gardens in general, the first flower of the year; and for this reason and its own charm of modest beauty, it will always be one of the best loved of our garden flowers".

*　　*　　*

In early March many and lovely are the flowering bulbs, and among them a wealth of blue, the more precious that it is the colour least frequent among flowers. The blue of scilla sibirica, like all blues that have in them a suspicion of green, has a curiously penetrating quality; the blue of scilla bifolia does not attack the eye so smartly. Chionodoxa sardensis is of a full and satisfying colour, that is enhanced by the small space of clear white throat. A bed of it shows very little variation in colour. Chionodoxa luciliæ, on the other hand, varies greatly; one may pick out light and dark blue, and light and dark of almost lilac colour

*　　*　　*

Leucojum vernum, with its clear white flowers and polished dark green leaves, is one of the gems of early March; and flowering at the same time, no flower of the whole year can show a more splendid and sumptuous colour than the purple of iris reticulata. Varieties have been raised, some larger, some nearer blue, and some reddish purple, but the type remains the best garden flower.

*　　*　　*

Where and how the early flowering bulbs had best be planted is a question of some difficulty. Perhaps the mixed border, where they are most usually put, is the worst place of all, for when in flower they only show as forlorn little patches of bloom rather far apart, and when their leaves die down, leaving their places looking empty, the ruthless spade or trowel stabs into them when it is desired to fill the space with some other plant. Moreover, when the border is manured and partly dug in the autumn, it is difficult to avoid digging up the bulbs just when they are in full root-growth. Probably the best plan is to devote a good space of cool bank to small bulbs and hardy ferns, planting the ferns in such groups as will leave good spaces for the bulbs.

*   *   *

"Probably the best plan is to devote a good space of cool bank to small bulbs and hardy ferns, planting the ferns in such groups as will leave good spaces for the bulbs".

Through April and May the leaves of the bulbs are growing tall, and their seed-pods are carefully removed to prevent exhaustion. By the end of May the ferns are throwing up their leafy crooks; by June the feathery fronds are displayed in all their tender freshness; they spread over the whole bank, and we forget that there are any bulbs between. By the time the June garden, whose western boundary it forms, has come into fullest bloom it has become a completely furnished bank of fern-beauty.

Violets

What a charm there is about the common dog-tooth violet; it is pretty everywhere, in borders, in the rock-garden, in all sorts of corners. But where it looks best with me is in a grassy place strewn with dead leaves, under young oaks, where the garden joins the copse. This is a part of the pleasure-ground

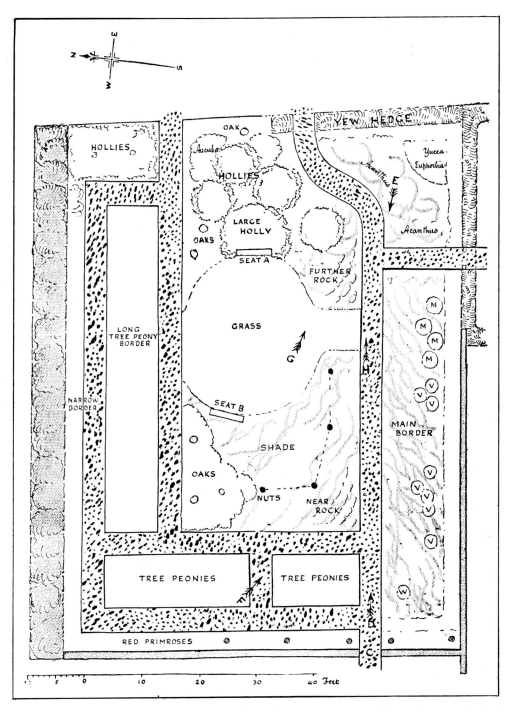

"A complete little garden of spring flowers. It begins to show some bloom by the end of March, but its proper season is the month of April and three weeks of May... In many places the spring garden has to give way to the summer garden, a plan that greatly restricts the choice of plants, and necessarily excludes some of the finest flowers of the early year".

"With April the spring flowers come crowding in. Planted dry walls and rock gardens this month and next are full of bloom".

that has been treated with some care, and has rewarded thought and labour with some success, so that it looks less as if it had been planned than as if it might have come naturally.

*   *   *

Violets must be replanted every year. When the last rush of bloom in March is over, the plants are pulled to pieces, and strong single crowns from the outer edges of the clumps, or from the later runners, are replanted in good, well-manured soil, in such a place as will be somewhat shaded from summer sun. There should be eighteen inches between each plant, and as they make their growth, all runners should be cut off until August. They are encouraged by liberal doses of liquid manure from time to time, and watered in case of drought; and the heart of the careful gardener is warmed and gratified when friends, seeing them at midsummer, say (as has more than once happened), "What a nice batch of young hollyhocks!"

The spring garden

As my garden falls naturally into various portions, distinct enough from each other to allow of separate treatment, I have found it well to devote one space at a time, sometimes mainly, sometimes entirely, to the flowers of one season of the year.

*   *   *

My spring garden lies at the end and back of a high wall that shelters the big summer flower border from the north and north-west winds. The line of the wall is continued as a yew hedge that in time will rise to nearly the same height, about eleven feet. At the far end the yew hedge returns to the left so as to fence in the spring flowers from the east and to hide some sheds. The space also encloses some beds of tree paeonies and a plot of grass, roughly circular in shape, about eight yards across, which is nearly surrounded by oaks, hollies and cob-nuts. The plan [overleaf] shows its disposition. It is of no design; the space was accepted with its own conditions, arranged in the simplest way as to paths, and treated very carefully for colour. It really makes as pretty a picture of spring flowers as one could wish to see.

The chief mass of colour is in the main border. The circles marked V and M are strong plants of veratrum and myrrhis. Gardens of spring flowers generally have a thin, poor effect for want of plants of important foliage. The greater number of them look what they are — temporary makeshifts... But herbaceous plants of rather large growth with fine foliage in April and May are not many... The myrrhis is the sweet Cicely of old English gardens. It is an umbelliferous plant with large fern-like foliage, that makes early growth and flowers in the beginning of May. At three years old a well-grown plant is a yard high and across. After that, if the plants are not replaced by young ones, they grow too large, though they can be kept in check by a careful removal of the outer leaves and by cutting out some whole crowns when the plant is making its first growth.

"My spring garden ... is of no design; the space was accepted with its own conditions, arranged in the simplest way as to paths, and treated very carefully for colour..."

"... It really makes as pretty a picture of spring flowers as one could wish to see".

"Myrrhis is the sweet Cicely of old English gardens ... with large fern-like foliage, that makes early growth and flowers in the beginning of May".

The copse in March and April

In summer it is clothed below with bracken, but now it bristles with the bluish spears of daffodils and the buds that will soon burst into bloom. The early Pyrenean daffodil is already out, gleaming through the low-toned copse like lamps of pale yellow light. Where the rough path enters the birch copse is a cheerfully twinkling throng of the dwarf daffodil (n. nanus), looking quite at its best on its carpet of moss and fine grass and dead leaves. The light wind gives it a graceful, dancing movement, with an active spring about the upper part of the stalk. Some of the heavier trumpets not far off answer to the same wind with only a ponderous leaden sort of movement.

* * *

The glory of the copse consists in the great stretches of daffodils. Through the wood run shallow, parallel hollows, the lowest part of each depression some nine paces apart. Local tradition says they are the remains of old pack-horse roads; they occur frequently in the forest-like heathery uplands of our poor-soiled, sandy land, running, for the most part, three or four together, almost evenly side by side. The old people account for this by saying that when one track became too much worn another was taken by its side. Where these pass through the birch copse the daffodils have been planted in the shallow hollows of the old ways, in spaces of some three yards broad by thirty or forty yards long — one kind at a time... The planting of daffodils in this part of the copse is much better than in any other portions where there were no guiding track-ways, and where they were planted in haphazard sprinklings.

The scents of spring

There are balmy days in mid-April, when the whole garden is fragrant with sweetbriar. It is not "fast of its smell", as Bacon says of the damask rose, but gives it so lavishly that one cannot pass near a plant without being aware of its gracious presence. Passing upward through the copse, the warm air draws a fragrance almost as sweet, but infinitely more subtle, from the fresh green of the young birches; it is like a distant whiff of lily-of-the-valley. Higher still the young leafage of the larches gives a delightful perfume of the same kind. It seems as if it were the office of these mountain trees, already nearest the high heaven, to offer an incense of praise for their new life.

* * *

The sweetness of a sun-baked bank of wallflower belongs to April. Daffodils, lovely as they are, must be classed among flowers of rather rank smell, and yet it is welcome, for it means spring-time, with its own charm and its glad promise of the wealth of summer bloom that is soon to come.

* * *

"Daffodils . . . are now waving rivers of bloom, in many lights and accidents of cloud and sunshine full of pictorial effect".

"The end of April brings the poet's narcissus (jonquil pœticus), and its still better and later double kind; a flower unsurpassed for beauty and value".

The rock garden in April

The best thing now in the rock garden is a patch of some twenty plants of arnebia echinoides, always happy in our poor, dry soil. It is of the borage family, a native of Armenia. It flowers in single or double-branching spikes of closely-set flowers of a fine yellow. Just below each indentation of the five-lobed corolla is a spot which looks black by contrast, but is of a very dark, rich, velvety brown. The day after the flower has expanded the spot has faded to a moderate brown, the next day to a faint tinge, and on the fourth day it is gone. The legend, accounting for the spots, says that Mahomet touched the flower with the tips of his fingers, hence its English name of prophet-flower.

The upper parts of the rock garden that are beyond hand-reach are planted with dwarf shrubs, many of them sweetly scented either as to leaf or flower — gaultherias, sweet gale, alpine rhododendron, skimmias, pernettyas, ledums, and hardy daphnes. Daphne pontica now gives off delicious wafts of fragrance, intensely sweet in the evening.

Periwinkles and wallflowers

I am never tired of watching and observing how plants will manage not only to exist but even to thrive in difficult circumstances. For this sort of observation my very poor sandy soil affords me only too many opportunities. Now, on a rather cold afternoon in April, I go to a sheltered part of the garden, and almost at random place my seat opposite a sloping bank thinly covered with periwinkles. The bank is the northern flank of a mound of sand, thinly surfaced when it was made with some poor earth from a hedge-bank that was being removed. This place was purposely chosen for the periwinkles, in order to check their growth and restrain them from running together into a tight mat of runners, as they do so quickly if they are planted in better soil... There is something among them on the ground looking like bright crimson flower-buds, about an inch long. I look nearer and see that they are acorns, fallen last autumn from a tree that overhangs this end of the bank. The acorns have thrown off their outer shells, and the inner skin of a pale greenish-yellow colour when first uncased, has turned, first to pale pink and then to a strong crimson. The first root has been thrown out and has found its way firmly into the ground, though the acorn still lies upon the surface.

*   *   *

Between and among the lesser periwinkles on the northern bank are spaces where neighbouring wallflowers have shed their seed, and seedlings have sprung up. Some of these, evidently on the poorest ground, have branched all round without throwing up a stem, and look like stiff green rosettes pressed close to the earth. Others, a little more well-to-do, have stout stocky stems and dense heads of short, almost horny, dark-green foliage, with promise of compact but abundant bloom. Like the inhabitants of some half-

"A bank of spring-flowering alpine plants... In planting the rock garden it is a good plan to allot fairly long stretches of space to nearly related plants... This way of grouping ... will not only have the best effect but will have a distinct botanical interest".

barren place who have never been in touch with abundance or ease of life or any sort of luxury, they are all the more sturdy and thrifty and self-reliant, and I would venture to affirm that their lives will be as long again as those of any sister plants from the same seedpod that have enjoyed more careful nurture and a more abundant dietary. No planted-out wallflower can ever compare, in my light soil, with one sown where it is to remain; it always retains the planted-out look to the end of its days, and never has the tree-like sturdiness about the lower portions of its half-woody stem that one notices about the one sown and grown in its place.

Tulips

Tulips are the great garden flowers in the last week of April and earliest days of May... One of the best for graceful and delicate beauty is tulipa retro-flexa, of a soft lemon-yellow colour, and twisted and curled petals; then Silver Crown, a white flower with a delicate picotee-like thread of scarlet along the edge of the sharply pointed and reflexed petals. A variety of this called Sulphur Crown is only a little less beautiful. Then there is Golden Crown, also with pointed petals and occasional threadings of scarlet. Nothing is more gorgeous than the noble gesneriana major, with its great chalice of crimson-scarlet and pools of blue in the inner base of each petal. The gorgeously flamed parrot tulips are indispensable, and the large double Yellow Rose, and the early double white La Candeur.

"From the end of April to the middle of May, tulips are in full beauty... Beds have an informal edging of stachys lanata, one of the most useful of plants for grey effects. Through it come tulips in irregular patches".

Spring shrubs

Many flowering shrubs are in beauty in April. Andromeda floribunda still holds its persistent bloom that has endured for nearly two months. The thick, drooping, tassel-like bunches of bloom of andromeda japonica are just going over. Magnolia stellata, a compact bush some five feet high and wide, is white with the multitude of its starry flowers; individually they look half double, having fourteen to sixteen petals. Forsythia suspensa, with its graceful habit and tender yellow flower, is a much better shrub than f. viridissima, though, strangely enough, that is the one most commonly planted. Kerria, with its bright-yellow balls, the fine old rosy ribes, the Japan quinces and their salmon-coloured relative pyrus Maulleii, spiraea Thunbergi with its neat habit and myriads of tiny flowers, these make frequent points of beauty and interest.

*   *   *

Two wall-shrubs have been conspicuously beautiful during May; the Mexican orange-flower (choisya ternata) has been smothered in its white bloom, so closely resembling orange-blossom. With a slight winter protection of fir boughs it seems quite at home in our hot, dry soil, grows fast, and is very easy to propagate by layers. When cut, it lasts for more than a week in water. Piptanthus nepalensis has also made a handsome show, with its abundant yellow, pea-shaped bloom and deep-green trefoil leaves. The dark-green stems have a slight bloom on a half-polished surface, and a pale ring at each joint gives them somewhat the look of bamboos.

"A large bush of magnolia stellata, whose milk-white flowers may be counted by the thousand".

A wood ramble in April

It is a windy day in early April, and I take my camp-stool and wander into the wood, where one is always fairly in shelter. Beyond the first wood is a bit of wild forest-like land. The trees are mostly oaks, but here and there a Scotch fir seems to have straggled away from the mass of its fellows, and looks all the handsomer for its isolation among leafless trees of quite another character. The season is backward; it still seems like the middle of March, and the ground covering of dead leaves has the bleached look that one only sees during March and the early weeks of a late April. It is difficult to believe that the floor of the wood will, a month hence, be covered with a carpet whose ground is the greenery of tender grass and fern-like wild parsley, and whose pattern is the bloom of primrose and wild hyacinth. As yet the only break in the leafy carpet is made by some handsome tufts of the wild arum, just now at their best.

"The only break in the leafy carpet is made by some handsome tufts of the wild arum".

*   *   *

Where the undergrowth is not cut down at the usual few years' interval, every now and then one comes upon an old hazel with a trunk six inches thick, or perhaps with a sheaf of five or six thick stems. It is only when one sees it like this that one recognises that it is quite one of the most graceful of small trees. The stems have a way of spreading outward and arching from the very base, forming a nearly true segment of a shallow circle. The bark becomes rough after three years' growth, but before that age, except for a thin scurf of papery brown flakes, relics of an earlier skin, it is smooth and half polished, the colour varying from grey-green to a cool umber, with bands and clouds of a silvery quality.

It is difficult to believe that we are well into April, the season is so backward; with frosty nights and winds that appear to blow equally cold from all quarters. To-day the wind comes from the south, though it feels more like north-east. How cold it must be in northern France! Coming back through the fir wood, the path is on the whole well sheltered, yet the wind reaches me in thin thready little chilly draughts, as if arrows of cold air were being shot from among the trees. The wind-blown firs in the mass have that pleasant sound that always reminds me of a distant sea washing upon a shingly beach.

The sun is away on my front and left, and the sharp shadows of the trees are thrown diagonally across the path, where the sunlight comes through a half-open place. Farther along, for some fifty yards or more, the path is in shade, with still more distant stretches of stem-barred glints of sunny space. Here the fir-trunks tell dark against the mist-coloured background. It is not mist, for the day is quite clear, but I am on high ground, and the distance is of the tops of firs where the hillside falls steeply away to the north. Where the sun catches the edges of the nearer trunks it lights them in a sharp line, leaving the rest warmly dark; but where the trees stand in shade the trunks are of a cool grey that is almost blue, borrowing their colour, through the opening of the track behind me, from the hard blue cloudless sky. The trunks seen quite against the sunlight look a pale greenish-brown, lighter than the shadow they cast, and somewhat warmed by the sunlit dead bracken at their feet. When I move onward into the shade the blue look on the stems is gone, and I only see their true colour of warm purplish-grey, clouded with paler grey lichen.

*   *   *

Now I come to the fringe of a plantation of spruce fir some thirty years old. The trees meet overhead above the narrow cart-track, and looking in from outside in the late afternoon light it might be the mouth of a black-dark tunnel, so deep and heavy is the gruesome gloom. And indeed it is very dark, and in its depths strangely silent. It is like a place of the dead, and as if the birds and small wood beasts were forbidden to enter, for none are to be seen or heard. But about the middle of this sombre wood there is a slight clearing; a little more light comes from above, and I see by the side of the track on the hitherto unbroken carpet of dull dead-brown, some patches and even sheets of a vivid green, and quantities of delicate white bloom. And the sight of this sudden picture of daintiest loveliness, of a value all the greater for its gloomy environment, fills the heart with lively joy and abounding thankfulness.

It is the wood-sorrel, tenderest and loveliest of wood plants. The white flower in the mass has a slight lilac tinge; when I look close I see that this comes from a fine veining of reddish-purple colour on the white ground. White seems a vaguely-indefinite word when applied to the colouring of flowers; in the case of this tender little blossom the white is not very white, but about as white as the lightest part of a pearl. The downy stalk is flesh-coloured and half-transparent, and the delicately-formed calyx is painted with faint tints of dull green edged with transparent greenish buff, and is based and tipped with a reddish-purple that recalls the veining of the petals. Each of these has a touch of clear yellow on its inner base that sets off the bunch of tiny whitish stamens.

The brilliant yellow-green leaf is a trefoil of three broad little hearts, each joined at its point to the upright stalk by a tiny stalklet just long enough to keep the leaf-divisions well apart. In the young foliage the leaflets are pressed down to the stalk and folded together. The mature ones also fold and sleep at night. Each little heart does not fold upon itself, but each half is closely pressed against the half of its neighbour, so that the whole looks like a blunt three-winged arrow-head or bolt-head.

A few minutes more and I am out of the sombre spruces, and again in the more open woodland, full of song of bird and movement of free air. The wood-path, following a nearly level contour of the steep hillside, dips across a sudden transverse gully. It is an old dead road or pack-horse track, one of many that scar the hillsides and indent the heathery wastes. A forgotten road of a day long since gone by; probably never made and certainly never mended. Centuries ago slightly hollowed, first by foot of man and laden or ridden beast, then grown more wide and deep by side crumbling of sandy earth and sweeping wash of sudden storm-flood. In the steep descent of this old dead lane one can read the whole history of its making, down to the rich valley-bottom where the washed-down soil lies nearly level in a wide flattened

"The ferns named as in the fern walk are not its only occupants ... coming into bloom in May are some fine clumps of trillium, the valued gift of an American friend".

drift, whose record is written in the richer growth of tree and bush and the ranker depth of luscious grass and weed.

I sit at the edge of the hillside path, and look down the old lane . . . As I sit quite quiet I hear in the wood high up on my left some small animal hunting among the dead leaves. By the smallness of the sound it should be a field-mouse; the movement is not heavy enough for a weasel, still less for a stoat; it is the sound of an animal of less than three ounces weight. Now I move on to a place where some underwood has lately been cut, and then to where the ground is naturally open, a half-acre of wild turf on the sunny hillside, of the fine grasses native to the sandy soil, with occasional tufts of the pretty wood-sage that will flower in the full summer . . . Just above this open space is a low hedgerow of hazels, with still rising wooded ground above. What a pretty and pleasant place that wise rabbit has chosen for his "bury" as the country folk call it; at the foot of the low sandy bank, and where it is kept quite dry by the roots of the old hazels. Just above is a carpet of wild hyacinth backed by hollies, and a little garden of the same comes right up to his front-door, where a tuft or two is partly buried by some of his more recent works of excavation.

Wood plants

Where the oaks grow there is a blue carpet of wild hyacinth; the pathway is a slightly hollowed lane, so that the whole sheet of flower right and left is nearly on a level with the eye, and looks like solid pools of blue . . . The song of the nightingale and the ring of the woodman's axe gain a rich musical quality from the great fir wood. Why a wood of Scotch fir has this wonderful property of a kind of musical reverberation I do not know; but so it is. Any sound that occurs within it is, on a lesser scale, like a sound in a cathedral. The tree itself when struck gives a musical note. Strike an oak or an elm on the trunk with a stick, and the sound is mute; strike a Scotch fir, and it is a note of music.

"Bold plantings of Solomon's seal, then wild bracken and the bushy growths of the woodland".

In the copse are some prosperous patches of the beautiful North American wood-lily (trillium grandiflorum). It likes a bed of deep leaf-soil on levels or cool slopes in woodland, where its large white flowers and whorls of handsome leaves look quite at home. Beyond it are widely spreading patches of Solomon's seal and tufts of the wood-rush (luzula sylvatica), showing by their happy vigour how well they like their places, while the natural woodland carpet of moss and dead leaves puts the whole together.

"It must be some five-and-twenty years ago that I began to work at what I may now call my own strain of primroses... They are, broadly speaking, white and yellow varieties of the strong bunch-flowered or polyanthus kind, but they vary so much, in form, colour, habit, arrangement, and size of eye and shape of edge, that one year thinking it might be useful to classify them I tried to do so, but gave it up after writing out the characters of sixty classes!... Their time of flowering is much later than that of the true or single-stalked primrose ... and they are at their best in the last two weeks of April and the first days of May... The primrose garden is in a place by itself — a clearing half shaded by oak, chestnut and hazel. I always think of the hazel as a kind nurse to primroses; in the copse they generally grow together, and the finest primrose plants are often nestled close into the base of the nut-stool".

Grouping flowers

I always think it desirable to group together flowers that bloom at the same time. It is impossible, and even undesirable, to have a garden in blossom all over, and groups of flower-beauty are all the more enjoyable for being more or less isolated by stretches of intervening greenery. As one lovely group for May I recommend Moutan paeony and clematis montana, the clematis on a wall low enough to let its wreaths of bloom show near the paeony.

* * *

I have a north wall eleven feet high, with a guelder rose on each side of a doorway, and a clematis montana that is trained on the top of the whole. The two flower at the same time, their growths mingling in friendly fashion, while their unlikeness of habit makes the companionship all the more interesting. The guelder rose is a stiff-wooded thing, the character of its main stems being a kind of stark uprightness, though the great white balls hang out with a certain freedom from the newly-grown shoots. The clematis meets it with an exactly opposite way of growth, swinging down its great swags of many-flowered garland masses into the head of its companion, with here and there a single flowering streamer making a tiny wreath on its own account.

* * *

May brings a wealth of bloom not only on hardy shrubs but on a number of good garden flowers. The old paeony (paeonia officinalis) should have a special place, in its three varieties of crimson, rosy red, and white. They are best in good masses accompanied by white flowers only — Solomon's seal, white columbine, and little bushes of deutzia gracilis and olearia Gunniana, and they may well be backed by the white Portugal broom which flowers at the same time.

"Among paeonies there is a preponderance of pink or rose-crimson colouring of decidedly rank quality, yet the number of varieties is so great, that among the minority of really good colouring there are plenty to choose from, including a good number of beautiful white and whites tinged with yellow".

95

Rhododendrons

Now, in the third week of May, rhododendrons are in full bloom on the edge of the copse. The plantation was made about nine years ago, in one of the regions where lawn and garden were to join the wood. During the previous blooming season the best nurseries were visited and careful observations made of colouring, habit, and time of blooming. The space they were to fill demanded about seventy bushes, allowing an average of eight feet from plant to plant — not seventy different kinds, but, perhaps, ten of one kind, and two or three fives, and some threes, and a few single plants, always bearing in mind the ultimate intention of pictorial aspect as a whole. In choosing the plants and in arranging and disposing the groups these ideas were kept in mind: to make pleasant ways from lawn to copse; to group only in beautiful colour harmonies; to choose varieties beautiful in themselves; to plant thoroughly well, and to avoid overcrowding. Plantations of these grand shrubs are generally spoilt or ineffective, if not absolutely jarring, for want of attention to these simple rules. The choice of kinds is now so large, and the variety of colouring so extensive, that nothing can be easier than to make beautiful combinations, if intending planters will only take the small amount of preliminary trouble that is needful. Some of the clumps are of brilliant scarlet-crimson, rose and white, but out of the great choice of colours that might be named only those are chosen that make just the colour-harmony that was intended. A large group, quite detached from this one, and more in the shade of the copse, is of the best of the lilacs, purples and whites. When some clumps of young hollies have grown, those two groups will not be seen at the same time, except from a distance.

*　　*　　*

A detail of pictorial effect that was aimed at, and that has come out well, was devised in the expectation that the purple groups would look richer in the shade, and the crimson ones in the sun. This arrangement has answered admirably. Before planting, the ground, of the poorest quality possible, was deeply trenched, and the rhododendrons were planted in wide holes filled with peat, and finished with a comfortable "mulch" or surface-covering of farmyard manure. From this a supply of grateful nutriment was gradually washed into the roots. This beneficial surface-dressing was renewed every year for two years after planting, and even longer in the case of the slower growing kinds. No plant better repays care during its early years.

Queen wasps

May is the time to look out for the big queen wasps and to destroy as many as possible. They seem to be specially fond of the flowers of two plants, the large perennial cornflower (centaurea montana) and the common cotoneaster. I have often secured a dozen in a few minutes on one or other of these plants, first knocking them down with a battledore.

"Among the various ways of passing from garden to woodland one of the best is by a planting of rhododendron ... Though the rhododendron is a mass of coloured bloom in early summer, yet ... they have the dark foliage and high polish that is so good in the winter months".

"In choosing the rhododendron plants and in arranging and disposing the groups these ideas were kept in mind: to make pleasant ways from lawn to copse; to group only in beautiful colour harmonies; to choose varieties beautiful in themselves, to plant thoroughly well, and to avoid overcrowding".
E. Wake Cook, "Rhododendron dell".

Spring flowers for decoration

The second half of March brings the strongest bloom of violets. Even a very few violets will scent a whole room. They are most manageable if they are arranged in the hand with all the ends of the stalks even, so that the heads are uneven; a few leaves should be picked and put among them. A bunch of violets is at its least beautiful in the form usually seen in shops, with the flowers all brought to one level and ringed with a stiff frill of leaves. Then when a few bunches are brought indoors, the ties should be relaxed. The old-fashioned heavy cut finger-glasses, with a glass tumbler stood inside, are capital things for holding them.

It is worth cutting a few branches of the red-leaved plum, prunus pissardi, when in young bud. If they are placed in water in a warm greenhouse, they soon open prettily, and are ready for use in the house. Peach prunings can be bloomed in the same way some weeks earlier.

"Spring flowers in Munstead glasses ... it is important to observe the way of growth of the flower in relation to the thing that is to hold it".

* * *

April and May hang together in the garden and therefore in its products for house decoration.

Fresh-picked wallflowers are delightfully sweet in rooms. Hardly any flower is more richly brilliant under articifial light than the so-called blood red colourings. The purples are beautiful arranged with white tulips. The purples and browns mingle very pleasantly in the sunlight of the spring garden, though this combination indoors is rather too heavy.

Care should be taken to strip off most of the leaves of cut wallflowers that will be under water, as they quickly decay, and the water should be often changed, for it soon becomes offensive. This is the case with stock also and with flowers of the cruciferæ in general. They belong to the same tribe as cabbages, and most people know only too well the bad smell of decaying cabbage leaves.

"I always think that this, the time of tulips, is the season of the year when the actual arranging of flowers affords the greatest pleasure".

* * *

The most beautiful flowering shrub of April is the neat and pretty magnolia stellata. A well-established plant is above six feet high and through, and bears its milk-white bloom in the greatest profusion. It grows so freely that whole branches can be cut, each branch having many flowers. These alone, or with some sprays of pyrus japonica, are charming in rooms, and look especially well in silver bowls.

Daffodils are in profusion in the earlier weeks of April, and towards the middle of the month berberis aquifolium is in bloom. In this state it arranges well with the largest daffodils.

I always think that this, the time of tulips, is the season of all the year when the actual arranging of flowers affords the greatest pleasure. The rush and heat of summer have not yet come; the days are still fairly restful, and one is so glad to greet and handle these early blossoms. There are not as yet too many flowers ... Moreover, the early flowers that come on slowly last long in water ... [and] the steadfast tulips will last for nearly a week, thus giving a better return for the time devoted to them.

*　　*　　*

Among tulips the most refined of form is the clear pale yellow t. retroflexa; with its sharp-pointed turned-back petals. This remarkable tulip is one of the most graceful of its kind; its freedom of form, and one might almost say freedom of action, making it quite unlike any other. Parrot tulips have something of the same habit as to wayward contortion of stem. This makes them a little difficult to arrange, but, when cleverly placed so that the weight of the heavy head is adequately carried, and the flower poised in accordance with the action of the stalk, the effect is excellent.

*　　*　　*

Pansies are not so often grown for indoor use as they deserve; perhaps because people do not think of the best way of using them. This is to cut, not the bloom only, but the whole shoot. When fair-sized sorts are grown, they can be cut nine inches long. They are delightful in wide bowls with the colours properly assorted, as white and yellow, white and blue, or white and purple together, and the rich and pale purples mixed; and the rich browns of the wallflower colours, either with or without the deeper yellows.

Then let anyone try a bowl of woodruff and forget-me-not, with a few pure white pansies; and enjoy, not their pleasant fresh colouring only, but their faint perfumes, so evenly balanced and so kindly blending.

The last fortnight of May brings the lilacs, now in many beautiful varieties, thanks to the unceasing labours of some of the best nurserymen of France. The whites are always beautiful alone, but white and lilac, especially those of the pinkish tinge, such as the one named Lucie Baltet, are charming together. One of the best whites, and one of the easiest to grow is Marie Legraye.

*　　*　　*

The end of May brings the first of the tree paeonies. They cannot be cut with long stalks as in the case of the herbaceous kinds, and therefore are best arranged in something of large bowl form. I have a very large and heavy old glass *tazza* that holds them well. They are pretty with some early sprays of clematis montana.

"The last fortnight of May brings the lilacs, now in many beautiful varieties... The whites are always beautiful alone".

"Tree paeonies cannot be cut with long stalks ... and are therefore best arranged in something of large bowl form... They are pretty with some early sprays of clematis montana".

Spring wild flowers in the house

"What an innocent charm there is about many of the true spring flowers".
W. Curtis, "Neapolitan Star of Bethlehem", from The Botanical Magazine.

By March there are the handsome leaves of lords-and-ladies, the wild arum . . . if wild daffodils can be found, they go well together; but the arum leaves are good alone, and there will still be some clusters of the heavy blackish-green ivy berries. Soon after the middle of the month is the time to look for the wild sweet violets, in the edges of copses or in low sunny hedge-banks; and in places where the small periwinkle grows, its pretty flowers may now be found.

*   *   *

March is the real time for the beauty of mistletoe. When it is gathered for Christmas the berries are not yet mature; in fact, they are not fully ripe till April. But a nice branch or two, put in water with some dark-berried ivy, will show its curious and quite special beauty to much advantage; and if some shoots of catkined palm-willow are added, either when the catkins are in their early dress of grey velvet or their later garb of yellow anther, the bouquet becomes still more interesting.

*   *   *

April brings the ever-welcome primroses, and on loamy soils cowslips. In the primrose woods will be wood anemones. They appear to wither before one can bring them home, but a deep bath will revive them. In damp meadows and the edges of withy and alder beds there will be marsh marigolds, and in cool meadows, in a few districts, the purple fritillaries. When the young green leaves come on the larch, little branches should be picked and arranged in water indoors for their delicious sweetness.

*   *   *

In May there are bluebells in the woods, and the early purple orchis with its splendid red-purple colouring; and young oak leaves, golden-green, and for handsome foliage quite young plants of burdock (arctium) . . . In the end of May we have the beginning of a class of plants that will add greatly to the beauty of our bouquets throughout the summer. These are various species of the umbelliferæ, common plants by all waysides. The earliest is the upright hedge parsley. They are so numerous and, to the non-botanical observer, so puzzling that I will not attempt to distinguish them. The thing that is most helpful is to advise that they should not be overlooked. They are plants of the parsley, carrot and cow-parsnip character, flowering in umbels and common everywhere; following each other until the autumn, so that there is always a good supply.

Summer

The gladness of June

What is one to say about June — the time of perfect young summer, the fulfilment of the promise of the earlier months, and with as yet no sign to remind one that its fresh young beauty will ever fade? For my own part I wander up into the wood and say, "June is here — June is here; Thank God for lovely June!" ... The soft cooing of the wood-dove, the glad song of many birds, the flitting of butterflies, the hum of all the little winged people among the branches, the sweet earth-scents — all seem to say the same, with an endless reiteration, never wearying because so gladsome.

Sweet peas

Within the first days of June we can generally pick some sweet peas from the rows sown in the second week of September. They are very much stronger than those sown in the spring. By November they are four inches high, and seem to gain strength and sturdiness during the winter; for as soon as spring comes they shoot up with great vigour, and we know that the spray used to support them must be two feet higher than for those that are spring-sown. The flower-stalks are a foot long, and many have four flowers on a stalk ...A few doses of liquid manure are a great help when they are getting towards blooming strength.

"Perfect young summer ... the flitting of butterflies, the hum of all the little winged people among the branches, the sweet earth scents". Hepzibah Abney, *"Summer grasses and butterflies".*

Poppies

"Munstead Cream Pink poppies resembling double paeonies . . . Poppies provide our gardens with beautiful and brilliant flowers in a great variety of form and colour".

Poppies provide our gardens with beautiful and brilliant flowers in a great variety of form and colour, both among the kinds that are of annual lifetime only and those that are perennial. Among the perennial kinds the earliest to bloom, flowering in the end of May and to the middle of June, is the Oriental group... An old but always useful form of p. orientale is known as bracteatum. The flowers are of a deeper scarlet than is usual among the ordinary kinds; by this and its stiff, upright habit it is most easily distinguished... P. rupifragum is a handsome plant with rough, hairy foliage much like that of orientale in miniature, and showy apricot-coloured flowers, carried singly on stems something over a foot high. It is useful in the flower border, but perhaps better in the rougher parts of rockwork. Another poppy of rather the same class but with smoother, more glaucous leaves, is p. pilosum. The flowers have nearly the same apricot colour, but there are several on a branching stem about two feet high; an almost daily removal of the spent blossoms will prolong the time of blooming. Both these poppies come freely from seed and should be renewed every two years, as they are not long-lived. The same thing, as to duration of lifetime, may be said of p. nudicaule... This pretty poppy, with flowers set singly on stems about a foot high, has yellow flowers in the type; but by cultivation and selection the colouring has both paled to white and deepened to full orange and red-lead colour. One of its most beautiful and refined tints is a pale yellow that may be called citron. This poppy is one of our hardiest plants, having wild homes well within the Arctic Circle. Papaver alpinum is a tiny form of the same plant; botanically inseparable from nudicaule. It has dainty, little, pale yellow flowers on stems three to four inches high, and finely divided foliage, and is a valuable rock plant.

*   *   *

Of the annual poppies, there are, first, the grand forms of the opium poppy (p. somniferum) in colourings of scarlet, pink, purple and white. Among the finest is one with wide guard petals, but is otherwise fully double, but not overcrowded. The colour is a full pink of a soft, creamy quality... Quite single poppies of this class are also handsome flowers, but are extremely fugacious... When the petals have fallen and the pod has swelled up a deep scratch or shallow cut on its surface is soon covered with a milky exudation, which dries a darker colour over the cut. This is opium in the rough.

*   *   *

It is almost impossible to sow poppies thinly enough, the seed is small, and even when mixed with three times its bulk of fine sand, the seedlings will come up much too thickly. They must be vigorously thinned; the great opium poppies must stand at least a foot apart — eighteen inches is none too much — and the lesser kinds in due proportion.

Cistuses

There can be little doubt that for the poor soils of our southern counties there are no better shrubs than the hardier of the cistuses. Of those that are hardy south of London the most easy to grow is c. laurifolius. It soon becomes a large bush; in sheltered places seven feet high and as much through. It will thrive in almost pure sand if deeply worked. Throughout the month of June it bears a daily succession of its two-inch-wide white flowers; it greets the kindly south-west wind with a lavish outpouring of its delicious fragrance, not only in summer but in the very depth of winter; and as it grows old, and here and there a branch breaks and dies, it has, like lavender and rosemary and juniper and many another good thing, an old age which is neither untidy nor unsightly but is dignified and pictorial.

Cistus ladaniferus, the gum cistus, is an even more beautiful shrub, but it is rather more tender. The manner of growth is not so solid or compact; the long shoots and long-shaped leaves look almost willow-like; but the beauty of the whole shrub is of a high order. So also is that of its wide white purple-blotched flowers of delicate substance, that, poppy-like, retain the mark of the folds of bud-life in the petals' dainty texture during their short span of unfolded beauty. For the only thing to regret about a cistus is that its flowers are so fugacious. Many expand in the morning to fall at noon, and though some may remain an hour or two later, yet by the afternoon the bushes are nearly bare, and only by the white pool of fallen petals on the ground below them may we know how fair and full was the flower of the forenoon.

"The only thing to regret about a cistus is that its flowers are so fugacious . . . by the afternoon the bushes are nearly bare, and only by the white pool of fallen petals on the ground below them may we know how fair and full was the flower of the forenoon".

"How good it is to
see the brilliant light
of the blessed summer
day, always brightest
just after rain, and to
see how every tree
and plant is full
of new life and
abounding gladness;
and to feel one's own
thankfulness of heart,
and that it is good to
live, and all the
more good to live
in a garden".
E.A. Rowe,
"Summer garden".

Roses and lilies

Apart from their high place of standing in our gardens and in our hearts, the rose and the lily are, of all familiar flowers, the two that for many centuries have been given a special degree of prominent distinction in matters altogether outside the domain of horticulture. For throughout the history of the civilised world within the last thousand years, the rose and the lily occur again and again, in closest bond with the most vital of human interests, and always in association with something worthy of fame or glory, whether in religion, in politics, or as devices of honour carried on the shields of those found worthy to bear them... And though the rose of England was not actually blazoned upon the shield of her kings, yet it has occurred so frequently among their badges that it is of distinct heraldic significance, and has stood for centuries as our national emblem.

*   *   *

Throughout our gardens there are many plants which are not botanically either roses or lilies, but because they are beautiful, and have a form that somewhat recalls that of these two kinds of flowers, the words rose and lily, with some other, either descriptive or qualifying, make up their popular name. So we have Christmas rose and Lenten rose for the flowers of the hellebore family that are so welcome from mid-winter to April; rock-rose and sun-rose for cistus and helianthemum, guelder rose for the white ball-flowers of the garden form of the water-elder, so good a shrub for many uses, not the least among these being as a wall-covering.

*   *   *

The word lily is still oftener used as a component of honour in the names of beautiful flowers both within and beyond the large botanical order of liliaceæ... So among our popular lily names we have lily-of-the-valley (convallaria), St. Bruno's lily (anthericum), arum lily (calla), African lily (agapanthus, one of the grandest of tub plants); Cape lily (crinum), splendid in its later developments; Amazon lily (eucharis). Then there is the beautiful belladonna lily (amaryllis), one of the noblest of pink-flowered plants and very sweet of scent... The lilies of France and the lily of Florence are, of course, irises, and indeed the beauty of this wonderful family entitles them to a place within the most exclusive aristocracy of flowers.

June: the time of roses

I have great delight in the best of the old garden roses; the Provence (cabbage rose), sweetest of all sweets, and the moss rose, its crested variety; the early damask, and its red and white striped kind... I am fond of the old rosa alba, both single and double, and its daughter, Maiden's Blush. How seldom one sees these roses except in cottage gardens; but what good taste it shows on the cottager's part, for what rose is so perfectly at home upon the modest little wayside porch?

I have also learnt from cottage gardens how pretty are some of the old

"Apart from their high place of standing in our gardens and in our hearts, the rose and the lily ... have been given a special degree of prominent distinction in matters altogether outside the domain of horticulture".

"The word lily is still oftener used as a component of honour in the names of beautiful flowers both within and beyond the large botanical order of liliaceae ... So among our popular lily names we have ... Cape lily, splendid in its later developments".

"I am fond of the old rosa alba ... how seldom one sees these roses except in cottage gardens; but what good taste it shows on the cottager's part, for what rose is so perfectly at home upon the modest little wayside porch?"

"I have some big round-headed standards, the heads a yard through ... that are worth looking at ... "

" ... though one of them is rather badly shaped this year, for my handsome Jack ate one side of it".

roses grown as standards. The picture of my neighbour, Mrs. Edgeler, picking me a bunch from her bush, shows how freely they flower, and what fine standards they make. I have taken the hint, and have now some big round-headed standards, the heads a yard through, of the lovely Celeste and of Madame Plantier, that are worth looking at, though one of them is rather badly-shaped this year, for my handsome Jack (donkey) ate one side of it when he was waiting outside the studio door, while his cart-load of logs for the ingle fire was being unloaded.

What a fine thing, among the cluster roses, is the old Dundee rambler! I trained one to go up a rather upright green holly about twenty-five feet high, and now it has rushed up and tumbles out at the top and sides in masses of its pretty bloom. It is just as good grown as a "fountain", giving it a free space where it can spread at will with no training or support whatever. These two ways I think are much the best for growing the free, rambling roses. In the case of the fountain, the branches arch over and display the flowers to perfection; if you tie your rose up to a tall post or train it over an arch or pergola, the birds flying overhead have the best of the show. The garland rose, another old sort, is just as suitable for this kind of growth as Dundee rambler, and the individual flowers, of a tender blush-colour, changing to white, are even more delicate and pretty... It is well worth getting up at 4 A.M. on a mid-June morning to see the tender loveliness of the newly opening buds; for, beautiful though they are at noon, they are better still when just awaking after the refreshing influence of the short summer night.

*   *   *

The newer crimson rambler is a noble plant for the same use, in sunlight gorgeous of bloom, and always brilliant with its glossy bright-green foliage. Of the many good plants from Japan, this is the best that has reached us of late years. The Himalayan rosa Brunonis is loaded with its clusters of milk-white bloom, that are so perfectly in harmony with its very long, almost blue leaves. But of all the free-growing roses, the most remarkable for rampant growth is r. polyantha. One of the bushes in this garden covers a space thirty-four feet across — more than a hundred feet round. It forms a great fountain-like mass, covered with myriads of its small white flowers, whose scent is carried a considerable distance. Directly the flower is over it throws up rods of young growth eighteen to twenty feet long; as they mature they arch over, and next year their many short lateral shoots will be smothered with bloom.

*   *   *

Now we look for the bloom of the burnet rose (rosa spinosissima), a lovely native plant, and its garden varieties, the Scotch briars. The wild plant is widely distributed in England, though somewhat local. It grows on moors in Scotland, and on Beachy Head in Sussex, and near Tenby in South Wales, favouring wild places within smell of the sea. The rather dusky foliage sets off the lemon-white of the wild, and the clear white, pink, rose and pale yellow of the double garden kinds. The hips are large and handsome, black and glossy, and the whole plant in late autumn assumes a fine bronzy colouring between ashy black and dusky red. Other small old garden roses are coming into bloom. One of the most desirable, and very frequent in this district, is rosa lucida, with red stems, highly-polished leaves, and single, fragrant flowers of pure rosy-pink colour. The leaves turn a brilliant yellow in autumn, and after they have fallen the bushes are still bright with the

"One of the many ways in which the splendid enthusiasm for good gardening — an enthusiasm which only grows stronger as time goes on — is showing itself, is in the general desire to use beautiful roses more worthily ... Now that there is such good and wonderfully varied material to be had, it is all the more encouraging to make rose gardens more beautiful ... to consider the many different ways in which roses not only consent to grow but in which they live most happily and look their best".
G.S. Elgood, *"Levens: Roses and pinks"*.

"Of the old cluster roses, the one I have found the prettiest and most generally useful is the garland, for it is beautiful in all ways, on arches ... for covering an arbour, or best of all as a natural fountain ... Year after year its graceful branches spring up and arch over and are fully laden with the lovely clusters of pink-white bloom".

"The Himalayan rosa Brunonis is loaded with its clusters of milk white bloom, that are so perfectly in harmony with its very long, almost blue leaves".

"The burnet rose is found ... generally in heathy places not very far from the sea. Among its many merits the beauty of its large, round, black hips should not be forgotten. These are like exaggerated black-currants, only more flattened at the poles".

coloured stems and the large clusters of bright red hips. It is the St. Mark's rose of Venice, where it is usually in flower on St. Mark's Day, April 25th. The double variety is the old rose d'amour, now rare in gardens; its half-expanded bud is perhaps the most daintily beautiful thing that any rose can show.

*   *   *

Blanc Double de Coubert is one of the best of roses, for it blooms the whole summer through and well into autumn. Its rich, deep green foliage, highly polished though heavily reticulated, persisting till late in the year, gives it that look of perfect health and vigour that the leafage of so many roses lacks in the later summer. The danger in rugosa hybrids is the tendency towards a strong magenta colouring, such as is suggested by the type... The great hardiness of the rugosas enables them to be used in exposed places where many kinds of roses would be crippled or would perish. Their strong, bushy growth and somewhat ferocious armature of prickles fits them above all other roses for use as hedges, and not hedges of ornament only, but effective hedges of enclosure and defence.

*   *   *

I do not think there is any other rose that has just the same rich butter colour as the yellow Banksian, and this unusual colouring is the more distinct because each little rose in the cluster is nearly evenly coloured all over, besides being in such dense bunches. The season of bloom is very short, but the neat polished foliage is always pleasant to see throughout the year. The white kind and the larger white are both lovely as to the individual bloom, but they flower so much more shyly that the yellow is much the better garden plant.

Ways with free-growing roses

For places where garden joins rougher ground or well-established shrubbery, especially if the shrubbery is mainly of evergreens such as box, yew, holly or ilex; by training a good selection of these roses among and through and over the dark-leaved shrubs a surprising number of delightful pictures of free rose growth and bloom may be produced; moreover the roses when encouraged to grow in this way, and when once established, seem to take the matter into their own hands; for I have noticed that they do their climbing in several different ways; some will run a little way up the supporting tree or bush and then shoot out the flowering branches, draping the tree's whole surface, while others ... will rush up the whole length of twenty feet or more and throw out a great crown of bloom around the top.

"Rosa Flora growing into shrubs ... roses when encouraged to grow in this way, and when once established, seem to take the matter into their own hands".

"I had observed, when at one point, from a little distance, I could see in company the pure deep orange of the herring lilies with the brilliant blue of some full-blue delphiniums, how splendid, although audacious, the mixture was, and immediately noted it, so as to take full advantage of the observation when planting-time came ... I could see already how grandly they went together, and how well worth doing and recommending such a mixture was".
G.S. Elgood, "Orange lilies and larkspur".

"For rambling through low tree growth and indeed any of the more free uses there are two roses, a red and a white, of extreme beauty, namely Reine Olga de Wurtemburg and Madame Alfred Carrière. Reine Olga will make shoots fifteen feet long in a season, and has the added merit of holding its admirable foliage in perfection for some weeks after Christmas. Madame Alfred Carrière, with its beautiful pale tea rose foliage and loose yellow-white bloom, soon becomes leggy below and is therefore all the more suitable for pushing up through bush and tree. The Boursaults delight in the same treatment, for it is exactly that of their alpine ancestor that grows on the fringes of woodland and in wild bushy tangles".

"There are roses that like nothing better than to trail over the ground, rising very little above it. Such a one is r. wichuraiana, neat and glossy of leaf and beauteous of its single white bloom. No plant is a better covering for a sunny sloping bank, and it seems almost more willing to grow down the bank than up it. I have a very neat growing South Italian form of r. sempervirens, with unusually glossy leaves, that a good deal resembles wichuraiana, and has a prostrate habit of nearly the same character, but this rose though of excellent foliage, enduring a good way through the winter, is very sparing of flower".

Rose arches

Many are the ways in which an arch of roses may be beautiful in the garden, whether it be a garden of some distinctly set design or one that is quite informal.

Where two ways meet or cross at a right angle there is always an opportunity for the placing of an arch of roses, or where flower garden passes into kitchen garden, whether it be walled or not. A rose arch is none the less a rose arch because there is a brick arch behind it, although what is generally understood as a rose arch is one that stands free or is in connection with a bounding hedge, the rose itself forming the arch, only supported by a framework of wood or iron.

But often in a modest garden there are other uses for a rose arch, such as the garden will itself suggest... A crimson rambler trained over a wire support in a free hedge of rhododendrons in a place where a path from one division of a garden leads into another. An incident in this picture [far right] that is not at all of unfrequent occurrence is worthy of notice. It is the carefully made rabbit-proof iron fencing, with two wires out in the lower part of the gate, leaving a space which seems to invite the entrance of any small animal. When it is desired to keep out rabbits, and an expensive fence is put up for this purpose, one such oversight makes the whole thing useless. Gates of this slight construction, which are in themselves perhaps the least distressing to the eye of all their unsightly class, are especially liable to injury from an accidental kick, or a blow from a barrow wheel.

Wrought iron gates, with richly designed ornament of the best kind that are made for the place itself, of perfect proportion and suitable enrichment, may well lead into and out of the rose garden, or indeed any other garden division, and roses may clamber near them, but it is more fitting that they should not climb over or into gates or screens of this class. Two such richly decorated objects as the artist-craftsman's work in enduring metal and the clusters of living rose had better be seen and enjoyed separately. But in the case of a simple arch in a brick garden wall and a wrought-iron gate of very simple design ... the rose is a welcome and rightly placed addition to the garden picture.

Rose hedges

Roses of the free-growing kinds adapt themselves readily to the form of hedges. One has only to choose a rose of more or less vigour, according to the height required. The hedge or screen way of growing them has the merit of ease of access for training and pruning as well as that of giving close enjoyment of the living walls of flowers. The tendency of nearly all strong growing roses is to rush up and leave bare places below. A rose hedge should, if possible, have a free space on both sides, when this defect can be remedied in two ways; one by training the shoots in an arched form with the tips bent well down, and the other to tip some of the outer strong young shoots that

"What is generally understood as a rose arch is one that stands free or in connection with a bounding hedge, the rose itself forming the arch, only supported by a framework of wood or iron".

"Many are the ways in which an arch of roses may be beautiful in the garden".

"Often in a modest garden there are uses for a rose arch, such as the garden itself will suggest".

"Wrought iron gates, with richly designed ornament .. may well lead into and out of the rose garden ... and roses may clamber near them, but it is more fitting that they should not climb over or into gates or screens of this class".

115

"Many are the opportunities in the planning of gardens for having a screen or hedge all of roses. Sometimes it may occur as part of the rose garden design, but more often in some detached portion of the grounds . . . where a rose screen or hedge will not only hide the unsightliness, but will provide a thing beautiful in itself and that yields a large quantity of bloom for cutting".

spring from the base. If in July these are shortened about a third, instead of continuing their growth in length, their energy goes to strengthening the shortened piece that is left. This will then, the following season, be thickly set with flowering laterals that will clothe the lower part of the hedge.

*   *   *

The height of the rose hedge, as in all other matters of garden design, must be determined in relation to the proportion of the space it is to fill and the size and distribution of whatever may be within view. Nothing is gained by carrying it up to a great height. Eight or nine feet is in most cases the limit of desirable height, while anything from four to seven feet will be likely to suit the wants of most modest gardens. A charming hedge four feet high can be made with the old favourite Madame Plantier. It is all the prettier if there is a short standard of the same at regular intervals.

Roses for converting ugliness to beauty

No plant is more helpful and accommodating than the rose in the way of screening ugliness and providing living curtains of flowery drapery for putting over dull or unsightly places. For instance, no object can be much less of an adornment to a garden than the class of ready-made wooden arbour or summer-house "made of well-seasoned deal, and painted three coats complete". Yet by covering it with an outer skin of ramping roses it may in about three years be made a beautiful thing, instead of an eyesore . . . Not only will it be beautiful, but the deep masses of leafy and flowery branches will keep off the sun-heat, which, without such a shield, makes these small wooden buildings insufferably hot in summer.

*   *   *

"What a splendid exercise it would be if people would only go round their places and look for all the ugly corners, and just think how they might be made beautiful by the use of free-growing roses . . . [such as a] climbing rose covering an old farm shed".

"There is no end to the beautiful ways of making rose arbours and tunnels ... An old dead apple tree, if it happens to stand where an arbour is wanted, need not even be moved; another bit of trunk can be put up to eight feet away, and the branches of the standing one sawn off, all but those that go the right way ... The roses seem to delight in such a rough built arbour, for they rush up and clothe it with most cheerful willingness".

"Dead or unprofitable old orchard trees, too, may have their smaller branches sawn off and planted with roses ... When once these roses get hold and grow vigorously the amount of their yearly growth is surprising".

Dead or unprofitable old orchard trees, too, may have their smaller branches sawn off and be planted with roses. If they are shaky, some stout oaken props, also rose-clothed, will steady them for many a year. When once these roses get hold and grow vigorously the amount of their yearly growth is surprising.

*   *   *

There is no end to the beautiful ways of making rose arbours and tunnels, or rose houses for the children. Dead trees or any rough branching wood can easily be put up and spiked together to make the necessary framework, and the roses will take to it gladly. An old dead apple tree, if it happens to stand where an arbour is wanted, need not even be removed; another bit of trunk can be put up eight feet away, and the branches of the standing one sawn off, all but those that go the right way. These branches can be worked in to form the top, keeping a stout, slightly curved piece for the front top beam. The roses seem to delight in such a rough built arbour, for they rush up and clothe it with the most cheerful willingness.

The back-door region and back-yard of many a small house may be a model of tidy dullness, or it may be a warning example of sordid neglect; but a cataract of rose bloom will in the one case give added happiness to the well-trained servants of the good housewife, and in the other may redeem the squalor by its gracious presence, and even by its clean, fresh beauty put better thoughts and desires into the minds of slatternly people.

*   *   *

What a splendid exercise it would be if people would only go round their places and look for all the ugly corners, and just think how they might be made beautiful by the use of free-growing roses. Often there is some bare yard, and it has come within my own experience to say to the owner, "Why not have rambling roses on these bare walls and arches?" and to have the answer, "But we cannot, because the yard is paved, or perhaps asphalted". Is not a grand rose worth the trouble of taking up two squares of flagging or cemented surface?

The madonna lily

A plant so lovely should be tried in every garden. It may be assumed as a general rule that where the soil is of loam, or of anything rich and holding, whether of a clayey or of a calcareous nature, that there it is likely to do well. Further than that we dare not go, for it is impossible to give a general prescription on several points of culture, such as whether to plant deep or shallow, whether to divide often or let alone, whether to manure or not; for, as the result of searching inquiry, we only get the most confusing and contradictory reports from persons whose observations are keen and accurate and whose statements may be accepted as absolutely trustworthy.

Thus, one good gardener says, "In every instance it resented manurial treatment in heavy soils." While another says, "Plant in rich soil well

"And the true lilies, the many lovely flowers comprised within the botanical family of lilium; what would our gardens be without them? Ever first and best comes the white or madonna lily (lilium candidum), emblem of spotless purity, and noblest and loveliest of garden flowers".

manured.'' Another ''L. candidum likes plenty of manure.'' As to soil, one writer says, ''I think our dry, open soil, saturated with iron, is the cause of bulbs being so healthy.'' Another says, ''In a hot, dry, old garden on a slope, the old madonna lily luxuriates; the rock is limestone, and there is a good deal of umber in the ground.'' On the one hand, the highest authority says, ''As to shade, we observe vigorous and healthy specimens of l. candidum growing year after year in a shady position'', and ''L. candidum likes general shade from buildings or trees ''... A distinguished amateur in Kent says, ''Few things have stood heat and drought so well as this lily.''

Then again we are told, ''In the heavy marsh land, with water very near the surface — a heavy clay that bakes hard in summer — the white lily flourishes.'' In Berkshire, where at the great house the gardener could not grow white lilies, they were grand in a near cottage (one of two) side by side, and failures in the next. The goodwife accounted for her flourishing lilies by saying that whereas her neighbour left the lilies dry, she watered hers copiously.

Then as to replanting; one says, ''Let alone four or five years''; another, ''Lift and divide every other year, and replant in fresh ground.'' On the Berkshire chalk downs an informant says, ''They have not been touched for twelve or fourteen years.'' From the South of France a successful grower writes, ''They have never been moved.'' Another at home says, ''Never disturb, but give a yearly top-dressing of rich compost''; and another, ''I have known them undisturbed for twenty years.''

The lesson taught by all these contradictions is, that every one must try how to grow the white lily in his own garden.

"Some of the lilies are of wonderful beauty in the woodland. In no other garden use are they seen to such advantage, for they seem to give of their best when they are given a place where there is surrounding of quiet conditions, and in some cases of isolation. Such a setting seems to be specially sympathetic to the stately lilium giganteum".

Some other lilies

The only lilies that do well in my poor soil are croceum, auratum, and tigrinum. Croceum is the early blooming orange lily that grows so well in London. It is the herring lily of the Dutch, blooming at the time when the great catches of herrings take place. I have got into the way of thinking of it and talking of it as the herring lily, and there are so many other lilies of an orange colour that for the sake of distinctness the name seems worthy of general adoption. Like other lilies long in cultivation, there are better and worse forms of it. The best one is a magnificent garden plant; in my borders, when full-grown, the third year after planting, it is seven feet high; a sumptuous mass of the deepest orange colour. When the bloom is over, it is cut away, and there are still left the stems of handsome foliage in regular whorls. But as I have it in the flower-border in rather large patches, and as by the late summer the mass of foliage, though wholesome and handsome, is a little too large and deep in colour, I grow behind it the white everlasting pea, training the long flowering shoots over and among the lily stems, with what seems to me the very happiest effect.

*   *   *

I had observed, when at one point, from a little distance, I could see in company the pure deep orange of the herring lilies with the brilliant blue of some full-blue delphiniums, how splendid, although audacious, the mixture was, and immediately noted it, so as to take full advantage of the observation when planting-time came. In the autumn, two of the large patches of lilies were therefore taken up and grouped in front of, and partly among, the delphiniums; and even though neither had come to anything like full strength in the past summer (the first year after removal), yet I could see already how grandly they went together, and how well worth doing and recommending such a mixture was. The delphiniums should be of a full deep-blue colour, not perhaps the very darkest, and not any with a purple shade.

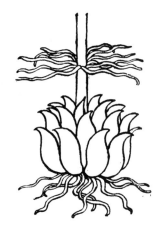

"Lily that makes stem roots, such as lilium auratum ..."

Tiger lilies also do well in well-prepared beds in my garden, the large variety "splendens" being the best and the tallest. Here they should be replanted at least every three years. By a poorer and smaller growth and an earlier yellowing of leaf, they show when they have exhausted the goodness of their bed and want it renewed. They bear numbers of bulbils in the axils of the leaves that can be grown on, and come to flowering size in about five years. It is a valuable lily, not only from its own beauty of free flower, black-spotted on salmon orange, of bold turn-cap shape, but because it is a true flower of autumn, blooming well into the third week of September. I always grow them in front of a yew hedge, the dark background of full, deep, low-toned green showing up their shape and colour to the fullest advantage.

The only other lily that I can depend on is lilium auratum... They are among rhododendrons in beds of peat and old hot-bed stuff. If the bulbs do not rot and die outright, or if the young shoots are not eaten off by mice in the spring, they make a fair growth the first year, and increase in strength for

" ... and one that makes no stem roots, such as lilium candidum".

some four or five years; after that they deteriorate. But by buying a case every two years, and picking out some of the best for pots and planting out the rest, I manage to keep up somewhat of an outdoor show. For some reason that those who know better than myself can perhaps explain, they flower over a very long period. The earliest will bloom in the end of June, and the latest in October.

One of the prettiest ways I have them is planted among groups of bambusa metake; in this way they scarcely want staking, and I always think look their very best. I was advised to do it by a friend who had seen them so grown in Japan, and I always feel grateful for the good advice when I see how delightfully they go together.

This fine lily, like some others, makes additional roots a little way up the stem. The roots thrown out by the bulb get to work first and prepare it for the effort of throwing up the flower stem. When this is a little way advanced, large hungry roots are thrown out from the stem itself, quite two inches above the bulb. This points to the need of deep planting, or better still, of planting first in a deep depression, and filling up later with a rich compost to such a depth as may leave these stem-roots well underground, for these are the roots that feed the flowers.

Midsummer

"Thou sentest a gracious rain upon thine inheritance; and refreshedst it when it was weary."

The whole garden is singing this hymn of praise and thankfulness. It is the middle of June; no rain had fallen for nearly a month, and our dry soil had become a hot dust above, a hard cake below. A burning wind from the east that had prevailed for some time, had brought quantities of noisome blight, and had left all vegetation, already parched with drought, a helpless prey to the devouring pest. Bushes of garden roses had their buds swarming with green-fly, and all green things, their leaves first coated and their pores clogged with viscous stickiness, and then covered with adhering wind-blown dust, were in a pitiable state of dirt and suffocation. But last evening there was a gathering of grey cloud, and this ground of grey was traversed by those fast-travelling wisps of fleecy blackness that are the surest promise of near rain the sky can show. By bedtime rain was falling steadily, and in the night it came down on the roof in a small thunder of steady downpour. It was pleasant to wake from time to time and hear the welcome sound, and to know that the clogged leaves were being washed clean, and that their pores were once more drawing in the breath of life, and that the thirsty roots were drinking their fill. And now, in the morning, how good it is to see the brilliant light of the blessed summer day, always brightest just after rain, and to see how every tree and plant is full of new life and abounding gladness; and to feel one's own thankfulness of heart, and that it is good to live, and all the more good to live in a garden.

The rain-drops still lodge in the grateful foliage. I like to see how the different forms and surfaces hold the little glistening globes. Of the plants

"An excellent place to grow auratum lilies is in rhododendron or azalea beds, or any bed where the soil is cool and peaty, and where the young growths will be protected by something bushy. In exposed gardens they suffer from the May frosts".

"In the flower border in July ... each one of the few flower-groups tells to the utmost, while the intervening masses of leafage are in themselves beautiful and have the effect of being relatively well disposed."

"The rain drops still lodge in the grateful foliage. I like to see how the different forms and surfaces hold the little glistening globes. Of the plants close at hand the way of the tree lupin is the most noticeable. Every one of the upright-standing leaves, like a little hand of eight or ten fingers, holds in its palm a drop more than a quarter of an inch in diameter".

close at hand the way of the tree-lupin is the most noticeable. Every one of the upright-standing leaves, like a little hand of eight or ten fingers, holds in its palm a drop more than a quarter of an inch in diameter. Each leaflet is edged with a line of light; the ball of water holds together by the attraction of its own particles, although there is a good space between the leaflets, offering ten conduits by which one expects it to drain away. Quite different is the way the wet hangs on the woolly leaves of verbascum phlomoides. Here it is in long straggles of differently sized and shaped drops, the woolly surface preventing free flow. In this plant the water does not always seem to penetrate to the actual leaf-surface; occasionally it does and wets the whole leaf, but more usually, when the drops remain after rain at night, they are held up by the hairy coating. Many of these downy leaves seem to repel water altogether, such as those of yellow alyssum and the other tall mullein (v. olympicum), in whose case the water rolls right off, only lodging where there is a hollow or obstruction. The drops always look brightest on these un-wetting surfaces, and while rolling look like quicksilver.

"Every garden is now wanting a pergola, that pleasant shape of covered way that we have borrowed from Italy".

I much enjoy the pergola at the end of the sunny path. It is pleasant while walking in full sunshine, and when that sunny place feels just a little too hot, to look into its cool depth, and to know that one has only to go a few steps farther to be in shade, and to enjoy that little air of wind that the moving summer clouds say is not far off, and is only unfelt just here because it is stopped by the wall. It seems wonderfully dark at first, this gallery of cool greenery, passing into it with one's eyes full of light and colour, and the open-sided summer-house at the end looks like a black cavern; but on going into it, and sitting down on one of its broad, low benches, one finds that it is a pleasant subdued light, just right to read by.

Elder trees

I am very fond of the elder tree. It is a sociable sort of thing; it seems to like to grow near human habitations. In my own mind it is certainly the tree most closely associated with the pretty old cottage and farm architecture of my part of the country; no bush or tree, not even the apple, seems to group so well or so closely with farm buildings. When I built a long thatched shed for the many needs of the garden, in the region of pits and frames, compost, rubbish and burn-heap, I planted elders close to the end of the building and on one side of the yard.

"Flowering elder along the path from garden to copse ... If I were not already overdone with home industries, I should distil fragrant elder-flower water; but I let the berries ripen and make them into elder wine, a pleasant, comforting and wholesome drink for winter evenings".

Any one who is in close sympathy with flower and tree and shrub, and has a general acquaintance with nature's moods, could tell the time of year to within a few days without any reference to a calendar; but of all dates it seems to me that Midsummer Day is the one most clearly labelled, by the full and perfect flowering of the elder. It may be different in more northern latitudes, but in mine, which is about half way between London and the south coast, the Festival of St. John and the flowering of the elder always come together; and though other plants, blooming at other seasons, are subject to considerable variation in their time of flowering, scarcely any is noticeable in the elder. So that one may say that however changeable in their characters may be the other days most prominent in the almanac from their connection with Feasts of the Church or matters of custom, yet Midsummer Day always falls on the 24th June. Indeed I have often noticed that however abnormal may have been the preceding seasons, things seem to right themselves about the middle of this month.

The country people say that the roots of elder must never be allowed to come near a well, still less to grow into it, or the water will be spoilt. The young shoots are full of a very thick pith; we used to dry it in my young days, and make it into little round balls for use in electrical experiments. The scent of the flowers, especially wind-wafted, I think very agreeable, though they smell too strong to bring indoors.

The flower border in July

Towards the end of July the large flower border begins to show its scheme. Until then, although it has been well filled with growing plants, there has been no attempt to show its whole intention. But now this is becoming apparent. The two ends ... are of grey foliage, with, at the near end, flowers of pale blue, white and lightest yellow. The tall spikes of pale blue delphinium are over, and now there are the graceful grey-blue flowers of campanula lactiflora that stand just in front of the great larkspurs. At the back is a white everlasting pea, four years planted and now growing tall and strong. The over-blown flowers of the delphinium have been removed, but their stems have been left just the right height for supporting the growth of the white pea, which is now trained over them and comes forward to meet the pale blue-white campanula. In front of this there is a drift of rue, giving a beautiful effect of dim grey colour and softened shadow; it is crowned by its spreading corymbs of pale yellow bloom that all rise nearly to a level. Again in front is the grand glaucous foliage of sea-kale. A little further along, and towards the back, is a bush of golden privet, taking up and continuing the pale yellow of the rue blossom, and forming a kind of ground-work to a group of the fine mullein verbascum phlomoides now fully out. Just below this is a clump of the double meadowsweet, a mass of warm white flower-foam. Intergrouped are tall snapdragons, white and palest yellow. Then forward are the pale blue-green sword blades of iris pallida dalmatica that flowered in June. This is one of the few irises admitted to the border, but it is here because it has the quality, rare among its kind, of maintaining its great leaves in beauty to near the end of the year. Quite to the front are lower-growing plants of purest blue — the Cape daisy (agathea cœlestis) and blue lobelia.

"The picture is complete and satisfying ... There is also such rich promise of flower beauty to come that the mind is filled with glad anticipation, besides feeling content for the time being with what it has before it".

Now we pass to a rather large group of eryngium oliverianum, the fine kind that is commonly but wrongly called e. amethystinum. It is a deep-rooting perennial that takes three to four years to become strongly established. In front of this are some pale and darker blue spiderworts (Tradescantia virginica), showing best in cloudy weather. At the back is thalictrum flavum, whose bloom is a little overpast, though it still shows some of its foamy-feathery pale yellow. Next we come to stronger yellows, with a middle mass of a good home-grown form of coreopsis lanceolata. This is fronted by a stretch of helenium pumilum. Behind the coreopsis are achillea eupatorium and yellow cannas.

Now the colour strengthens with the scarlet balm or bergamot, inter-grouped with senecio artemisiæfolius, a plant little known but excellent in the flower border. A few belated orange lilies have their colour nearly repeated by the gazanias next to the path. The strong colour is now carried on by lychnis chalcedonica, scarlet salvia, lychnis haageana (a fine plant that is much neglected), and some of the dwarf tropæolums of brightest scarlet. After this we gradually return to the grey-blues, whites and pale yellows, with another patch of eryngium oliverianum, white everlasting pea, calceolaria, and the splendid leaf-mass of a wide and high plant of euphorbia Wulfenii, which, with the accompanying yuccas, rises to a height far above my head. Passing between a clump of yuccas on either side is the cross-walk leading by an arched gateway through the wall. The border beyond this is a shorter length, and has a whole ground of grey foliage — stachys, santolina, elymus, cineraria maritima, and sea-kale. Then another group of rue, with grey-blue foliage and pale yellow bloom, shows near the extreme end against the full green of the young summer foliage of the yew arbour that comes at the end of the border. Again at this end is the tall campanula lactiflora. In the nearer middle a large mass of purple clematis is trained over stiff, branching spray, and is beginning to show its splendid colour, while behind, and looking their best in the subdued light of the cloudy morning on which these notes are written, are some plants of verbascum phlomoides, ten feet high, showing a great cloud of pure pale yellow. They owe their vigour to being self-sown seedlings, never transplanted. Instead of having merely a blooming spike, as is the usual way of those that are planted, these have abundant side branches. They dislike bright sunshine, only expanding fully in shade or when the day is cloudy and inclined to be rainy. Close to them, rising to the wall's whole eleven feet of height, is a cistus cyprius, bearing a quantity of large white bloom with a deep red spot at the base of each petal.

Though there is as yet but little bloom in this end of the border, the picture is complete and satisfying. Each one of the few flower groups tells to the utmost, while the intervening masses of leafage are in themselves beautiful and have the effect of being relatively well disposed. There is also such rich promise of flower beauty to come that the mind is filled with glad anticipation, besides feeling content for the time being with what it has before it.

"The good old white pink ... as an edging plant we have not found anything better among flowering plants. The white pink is in fact a better thing than the larger modern kinds that in so many gardens have taken the place of the old favourite, one of whose many merits is its close habit and good silvery foliage in winter".

Filling gaps

There are certain classes of plants that are quite indispensable, but that leave a bare or shabby-looking place when their bloom is over. How to cover these places is one of the problems that have to be solved. The worst offender is Oriental poppy; it becomes unsightly soon after blooming, and is quite gone by midsummer. I therefore plant gypsophila paniculata between and behind the poppy groups, and by July there is a delicate cloud of bloom instead of large bare patches. Eryngium oliverianum has turned brown by the beginning of July, but around the group some dahlias have been planted, that will be gradually trained down over the space of the departed sea-holly, and other dahlias are used in the same way to mask various weak places.

Carnations

But the flower of July that has the firmest hold of the gardener's heart is the carnation — the clove gilliflower of our ancestors. Why the good old name "gilliflower" has gone out of use it is impossible to say, for certainly the popularity of the flower has never waned. Indeed, in the seventeenth century it seems that it was the best-loved flower of all in England; for John Parkinson, perhaps our earliest writer on garden plants, devotes to it a whole chapter in his "Paradisus Terrestris", a distinction shared by few other flowers. He describes no less than fifty kinds, a few of which are still to be recognised, though some are lost. For instance, what has become of the "*great gray Hulo*", which he describes as a plant of the largest and strongest habit? The "gray" in this must refer to the colour of the leaf, as he says the flower is red; but there is also a variety called the "*blew Hulo*", with flowers of a "purplish murrey" colouring, answering to the slate colour that we know as of not unfrequent occurrence ... But though some of the older sorts may be lost, we have such a wealth of good known kinds that this need hardly be a matter of regret. The old red clove always holds its own for hardiness, beauty, and perfume; its newer and dwarfer variety, Paul Engleheart, is quite indispensable, while the beautiful salmon-coloured Raby is perhaps the most useful of all, with its hardy constitution and great quantity of bloom. But it is difficult to grow carnations on our very poor soil; even when it is carefully prepared they still feel its starving and drying influence, and show their distaste by unusual shortness of life.

A little August garden

It has been a great pleasure and interest during recent years to make out a plan for a little garden of restricted colouring for the month of August, and it has met with so much appreciation and encouragement from those whose opinion I most value, and so much simple admiration from many who have no special understanding of colour combinations, but who cannot help seeing that it is pretty and distinctly effective, that I am now year by year trying to improve it in detail. The accompanying sketch of its general

"*Gypsophila paniculata between and behind the poppy groups ... by July there is a delicate cloud of bloom instead of large bare patches*".

arrangement will serve as a suggestion to any who may feel an interest in such a plan, and may like to continue the experiment for themselves. The colouring is of purple, pink and white flowers, with a good deal — in fact, a general setting — of grey foliage. The plants that make the greater part of the effect are a good clear pink hollyhock, clematis Jackmanii and a bright purple form of delphinium consolida. What may be called the secondary plants are snapdragons (pale pink and white), China asters (purple and white), and good double pink godetia, and purple and pink gladioli... The grey plants are the low-growing artemisia stelleriana at the angles, and a good deal of the tall a. ludoviciana in other parts of the border. This is a most accommodating plant, for it can be used up against the hollyhocks its full height of five feet, or it can be cut down to any height that may best suit its neighbours. Then there is the fine silvery white of the best form of cineraria maritima, and, for front edges, the ever-useful stachys lanata. Some well-grown plants of gypsophila paniculata, that spread to nearly four feet, also come in as grey colouring. As there are not many pink flowers available, I had hoped to use lavatera olbia in the back parts of the border... One lavatera only is shown on the plan, but more, if of the right kind, would be desirable. The dahlias are of the star kinds, white and cool pink.

"By far the most beautiful [hollyhock] is one of a pure pink colour, with a wide outer frill. It came first from a cottage garden and has always since been treasured. I call it Pink Beauty".

As with all other border gardening, it is not enough to plant and then expect it to do all that we wish without further care, for to have it right it must be constantly watched and guided and tended. The first thing will be to see that the clematis Jackmanii, which makes growth early, is trained in the right direction on pea-sticks in the case of those near the echinops, so that it will come just over it and finally lie on its tops when the colour of the globe thistle begins to go; for the clematis is much the longer lasting of the two... Some of the clematis are trained into the sea buckthorn (hippophaë); this is kept trimmed to a suitable height and gives the setting of grey foliage that is desired. The next duty will be to cut out the blooming shoots of the stachys,

"Many of the charming bell-flower family are fine things in the flower border ... Canterbury bells are well known and in every garden".
George S. Elgood, "Purple campanula".

for it is the carpet of silvery leaves that is wanted, not the lanky, ineffective bloom; as soon as this is cut away the plant spreads at the base. Then as the artemisia ludoviciana grows, it is topped and topped again at about fortnightly intervals, to make it do exactly as one wishes. The two annuals, the pink godetia and the delphinium consolida, are sown in place. After the first year the delphinium probably comes up self sown, but it is better to save selected seed and to sow early in March. As soon as flower buds show, the whole tops are cut off, and this cutting back is repeated till the middle of July. This is not only to make the plants bushy and more densely bloomed, but to keep them back till August.

"The fern-walk is at its best ... The mossy bank, some nine feet wide, and originally cleared for the purpose, is planted with large groups of hardy ferns".

"Among the thick masses of green bracken is a frond or two turning yellow. This always happens in the first or second week of August ... it is taken as a sign that the fern is in full maturity".

Bracken, heaths and ferns

Here and there in the copse, among the thick masses of green bracken, is a frond or two turning yellow. This always happens in the first or second week of August, though it is no indication of the approaching yellowing of the whole. But it is taken as a signal that the fern is in full maturity, and a certain quantity is now cut to dry for protection and other winter uses. Dry bracken lightly shaken over frames is a better protection than mats, and is almost as easily moved on and off.

The ling is now in full flower, and is more beautiful in the landscape than any of the garden heaths; the relation of colouring, of greyish foliage and low-toned pink bloom with the dusky spaces of purplish-grey shadow, are a precious lesson to the colour-student.

The fern-walk is at its best. It passes from the garden upwards to near the middle of the copse. The path, a wood-path of moss and grass and short-cut heath, is a little lower than the general level of the wood. The mossy bank, some nine feet wide, and originally cleared for the purpose, is planted with large groups of hardy ferns, with a preponderance (due to preference) of dilated shield fern and lady fern. Once or twice in the length of the bank are hollows, sinking at their lowest part to below the path-level, for osmunda and blechnum.

"In trying to work out beautiful garden effects, besides those purposely arranged, it sometimes happens that some little accident — such as the dropping of a seed, that has grown and bloomed where it was not sown — may suggest some delightful combination unexpected and unthought of".

"What is most to be desired in all decorative gardening is that it shall be fitting to its place. Every site, whether great or small, is capable of being suitably treated".

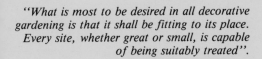

"Lavender has been unusually fine; to reap its fragrant harvest is one of the many joys of the flower year. If it is to be kept and dried, it should be cut when as yet only a few of the purple blooms are out on the spike; if left too late, the flower shakes off the stalk too readily".

Reserve plants

August is the time to begin to use our reserve of plants in pots. Of these the most useful are the hydrangeas. They are dropped into any vacant spaces, more or less in groups, in the two ends of the border where there is grey foliage, their pale pink colouring agreeing with these places. Their own leafage is a rather bright green, but we get them so well bloomed that but few leaves are seen, and we arrange as cleverly as we can that the rest shall be more or less hidden by the surrounding bluish foliage. I stand a few paces off, directing the formation of the groups; considering their shape in relation to the border as a whole. I say to the gardener that I want a hydrangea in such a place, and tell him to find the nearest place where it can be dropped in. Sometimes this dropping in, for the pots have to be partly sunk, comes in the way of some established plant. If it is a deep-rooted perennial that takes three or four years to come to its strength, like an eryngium or a dictamnus, of course I avoid encroaching on its root-room. But if it is a thing that blooms the season after it is planted, and of which I have plenty in reserve, such as an anthemis, a Tradescantia, or a helenium, I sacrifice a portion of the plant-group, knowing that it can easily be replaced.

Fruit from the garden

Surely my fruit garden would be not only a place of beauty, of pleasant sight and pleasant thought, but of leisurely repose, a repose broken only faintly and in welcome fashion by its own interests — in July, August and September a goodly place in which to wander and find luscious fruits in quantity that can be gathered and eaten straight from the tree. There is a pleasure in searching for and eating fruit in this way that is far better than having it ... set before one on a dish in a tame room. Is this feeling an echo of far-away days of savagery when men hunted for their food and rejoiced to find it, or is it rather the poet's delight of having direct intercourse with the good gift of the growing thing and seeing and feeling through all the senses how good and gracious the thing is? To pass the hand among the leaves of the fig tree, noting that they are a little harsh upon the upper surface and yet soft beneath; to be aware of their faint, dusky scent; to see the cracking of the coat of the fruit and the yellowing of the neck where it joins the branch — the two indications of ripeness — sometimes made clearer by the drop of honeyed moisture at the eye; then the handling of the fruit itself, which must needs be gentle because the tender coat is so readily bruised and torn; at the same time observing the slight greyish bloom and the colouring — low-toned transitions of purple and green; and finally to have the enjoyment of the luscious pulp, with the knowledge that it is one of the most wholesome and sustaining of fruit foods — surely all this is worthy garden service!

Summer flowers for decoration

The Oriental poppy began in May but may well be classed among June flowers. One often hears it said that this grand poppy will not live in water. This is by no means the case, though it is easy to see why it is so generally believed. Poppies, and some other flowers, have a milky juice which has the property of drying quickly. If they are cut and not put in water immediately, this juice dries and seals up the cut end of the stalk so that it cannot draw up water. The stalk should be freshly cut and also slit up the moment before it is put in the water; then the milky juice is washed away and the flowers live quite as long as any others of the time of year.

Guelder rose is charming arranged with clematis montana, and perhaps one or two of the rose-coloured herbaceous paeonies that will still be in bloom. These paeonies are in three colourings, deep crimson, rose-coloured, and a pale pink that fades to a dull white. Guelder rose and all other hard-wooded flowers should have their woody stems slit up, or a strip or two of the bark should be torn up for two or three inches. They naturally take up water with more difficulty than flowers with more fleshy stalks, and are therefore helped by any treatment that presents a larger expanse of raw tissue to the water.

*   *   *

"When the days are hot and long, and the earth is warm ... what a time of gladness it is".
George S. Elgood, "Crathes: Phlox" (detail).

"What, indeed, is more delightful than a silver bowl, or one of blue and white china, full of fresh roses!"

"White everlasting pea, one of the best and most enduring of July flowers".

In the last days of June there will be Canterbury bells. We grow them in three colours; white, pink and pale lilac for preference. They are admirable as cut flowers; no summer blooms last better in water. The cup-and-saucer variety is the best form; the outer frill or flounce enriching the flower. Canterbury bells can also be potted when just about to open, appearing to take no notice of what many people would consider a hazardous operation at so late a time of their life.

*   *   *

The first half of July brings the main bloom of roses. All kinds of roses, in their many ways, adapt themselves to good room treatment. There is a delightful freshness of sweet scent in a room newly decked with many roses, although some that are really sweet do not give off their perfume freely. They are "fast flowers of their smell", as Bacon says. But the warmth of a room brings out as much of the perfume as can be given off.

It may be taken as a general rule that the splendid blooms of the hybrid perpetuals are best arranged in low bowls.

*   *   *

Sweet Williams are grand flowers in early July and throughout the month. The strong, deep, velvety reds of scarlet quality have a richness of colouring that is hardly surpassed by any flower... But sweet Williams, fine though they are in the best colourings and markings, are not satisfactory in form by themselves. They want something of more upright shape to counteract the monotony of their flat heads. For this reason they are best in mixed bouquets, with roses, Canterbury bells, peach-leaved bell-flower, honeysuckle, pinks — any or all of these.

For large and tall arrangements we have the two sea hollies (eryngium oliverianum and e. giganteum); white foxgloves, delphiniums and the tall white variety of campanula lactiflora. This fine campanula, so seldom grown, is five feet high; it has large heads with a pyramidal outline of pretty bell-flowers of a pale grey-blue colour. Beautiful arrangements can be made of it with a groundwork of the glistening silvery eryngium giganteum (the silver thistle) whose rigid stiffness makes a helpful support, and another most useful campanula, the white variety of c. latifolia; the whole made brilliant with some sprays of white everlasting pea, one of the best and most enduring of July flowers.

*   *   *

Among the best of cutting flowers, beautiful and long-lasting, are the alströmerias, both the yellow and orange a. aurea, and in its better variety, a. aurantiaca, and the variously coloured a. chilensis. These vary in tinting, from pinkish white or flesh colour, through soft yellow, orange and charming shades of full and rosy pink, to red. All the colourings go well together. They have no effective foliage of their own, but look extremely well with a few bold leaves of funkia Sieboldi.

*   *   *

Sweet peas should be cut in whole sprays as well as in single blooms. The number of varieties is now so great that it is easy to choose from among them those that will make the best colour harmonies, such as lavender and white together, salmon and salmon red; rose, white and pale pink.

*　　*　　*

Lilies, whose smell is delicious in open-air wafts, cannot be borne in a room. In the south of Europe a tuberose cannot be brought indoors, and even at home I remember one warm wet August how a plant of balm of gilead (cedronella triphylla) had its always powerful but usually agreeably-aromatic smell so much exaggerated that it smelt exactly like coal-gas! A brother in Jamaica writes of the large white jasmine: "It does not do to bring it indoors here; the scent is too strong. One day I thought there was a dead rat under the floor (a thing which did happen once), and behold, it was a glassful of fresh white jasmine that was the offender!"

"August is the month of China asters. There is now a good range of kinds that yield long-stemmed flowers of free outline, quite admirable for indoor use".

Summer wild flowers in the house

June brings flowers in plenty. By the waterside the lovely forget-me-not, the yellow water iris and the great yellow loosestrife, and perhaps some bushes of the water elder, whose ball-flowered form is the guelder rose of our gardens. In meadows there will be marsh orchis and ragged Robin; near the sea the horned poppy, beautiful both of leaf and flower and the sea campion; on the edges of woodland foxgloves and the still more useful French willow (epilobium) ... On dry banks in light soil there will be broom and ox-eye daisies; on chalk the rosy-crimson saintfoin, handsomest of native plants of the vetch and clover family. In hedges there will be dog roses and elder in bloom — good to arrange together.

Now is the time of beautiful grasses. Every roadside and field footpath is bordered with them; there are only too many to choose from.

*　　*　　*

In July, perhaps the best flowers are to be found by the waterside. The leaves and spreading bloom of the great water plantain look like something from the tropics. A lucky search may find one or two blooms of the flowering rush (butomus) or of arrowhead.

In hedges and the more open parts of woodland there will be honeysuckle; in wood edges the tall bell-flower (campanula trachelium); in woodsides and hedges also three beautiful plants of the pea and bean tribe — namely, the pink rest-harrow, the large yellow meadow vetchling, and the purple tufted vetch.

In cornfields there will be cornflowers and viper's bugloss; in sandy places near the sea the sea-holly and the handsome sea-bindweed; on chalk the pale blue-flowered chicory, and in copses Daphne laureola; on heathland the pink bell-heather (erica tetralix), and perhaps in boggy places the sweet leaved bog-myrtle, and everywhere on dry banks the graceful hare-bells.

"A bouquet of wild flowers ... In June there will be dog roses and elder in bloom — good to arrange together ... In July ... in hedges and the more open parts of woodland there will be honeysuckle".

George S. Elgood. 1894

*e thinking out of ... details according to the conditions of the site, the combining of them
designs that shall add to its beauty, and the actual working of them, the mind meanwhile
ering the effect in advance — these are some of the most interesting and enlivening of the
kinds of happiness that a garden gives".* George S. Elgood, *"Bulwick: The gateway".*

"There is a double border for the month of September alone ... approached by an arch of laburnum ... The scheme of colouring consists of [a] groundwork of grey foliage, with white, lilac, purple and pale pink flowers; and, breaking into this colouring in two or three distinct places, flowers of pale yellow and yellowish white with suitable accompanying leafage".

"There is a place near my house where a path leads down through a nut walk to the further garden. It is crossed by a shorter path that ends at a birch tree with a tall silvered trunk".

Left, hydrangea tubs and the birch tree. Above, in the nut walk.

Autumn

An autumn scene

There is a place near my house where a path leads down through a nut walk to the further garden. It is crossed by a shorter path that ends at a birch tree with a tall silvered trunk. It seemed desirable to accentuate the point where the paths cross; I therefore put down four square platforms of stone "pitching" as a place for the standing of four hydrangeas in tubs. Just before the tree is a solid wooden seat and a shallow wide step done with the same stone pitching. Tree and seat are surrounded on three sides by a rectangular planting of yews. The tender greys of the rugged lower bark of the birch and the silvering of its upper stem tell finely against the dark velvet-like richness of the yew and the leaf-mass of other trees beyond; the pink flowers and fresh green foliage of the hydrangeas are also brilliant against the dusky green. It is just one simple picture that makes one glad for three months of the later summer and early autumn.

Hollyhocks

Hollyhocks have so long been favourite flowers — and, indeed, what would our late summer and autumn gardens be without them? ... The loosely-folded inner petals of the loveliest hollyhocks invite a wonderful play and brilliancy of colour. Some of the colour is transmitted through the half-transparency of the petal's structure, some is reflected from the neighbouring folds; the light striking back and forth with infinitely beautiful trick and playful variation, so that some inner regions of the heart of a rosy flower, obeying the mysterious agencies of sunlight, texture and local colour, may tell upon the eye as pure scarlet; while the wide outer petal, in itself generally rather lighter in colour, with its slightly waved surface and gently frilled edge, plays the game of give and take with light and tint in quite other, but always delightful ways.

"Hollyhocks have so long been favourite flowers — and, indeed, what would our late summer and autumn gardens be without them?"

"See how well the groups [of hollyhocks] have been placed; the rosy group leading to the fuller red, with a distant sulphur-coloured gathering at the far end; its tall spires of bloom shooting up and telling well against the distant tree masses above the wall".
George S. Elgood, *"Blyborough: Hollyhocks".*

"It was a pleasant thought, that of the lover of good flowers and firm friend of many good people, who first had the idea of combining the two sentiments into a garden of enduring beauty".
George S. Elgood, *"Stone Hall, Easton: The Friendship Garden, mid-September".*

September-sown annuals

In the second week of September we sow sweet peas in shallow trenches. The flowers from these are larger and stronger and come in six weeks earlier than from those sown in the spring; they come too at a time when they are especially valuable for cutting. Many other hardy annuals are best sown now. Some indeed, such as the lovely collinsia verna and the large white iberis, only do well if autumn-sown. Among others, some of the most desirable are nemophila, love-in-a-mist, larkspurs, pot marigold, Virginian stock, and the delightful Venus's navel-wort (omphalodes linifolia). I always think this daintily beautiful plant is undeservedly neglected, for how seldom one sees it. It is full of the most charming refinement, with its milk-white bloom and grey-blue leaf and neat habit of growth. Any one who has never before tried annuals autumn-sown would be astonished at their vigour. A single plant of nemophila will often cover a square yard with its beautiful blue bloom; and then, what a gain it is to have these pretty things in full strength in spring and early summer, instead of waiting to have them in a much poorer state later in the year, when other flowers are in plenty.

Dahlias

In September dahlias are at their full growth. To make a choice for one's own garden, one must see the whole plant growing. As with many another kind of flower, nothing is more misleading than the evidence of the show table, for many that there look the best, and are indeed lovely in form and colour as individual blooms, come from plants that are of no garden value. For however charming in humanity is the virtue modesty, and however becoming is the unobtrusive bearing that gives evidence of its possession, it is quite misplaced in a dahlia. Here it becomes a vice, for the dahlia's first duty in life is to flaunt and to swagger and to carry gorgeous blooms well above its leaves, and on no account to hang its head. Some of the delicately-coloured kinds lately raised not only hang their heads, but also hide them away among masses of their coarse foliage, and are doubly frauds, looking everything that is desirable in the show, and proving worthless in the garden. It is true that there are ways of cutting out superfluous green stuff and thereby encouraging the blooms to show up, but at a busy season, when rank leafage grows fast, one does not want to be every other day tinkering at the dahlias.

Begonias

Begonias are at their best throughout the month of September. Beds of begonias alone never seem to me quite satisfactory. Here there is no opportunity for growing them in beds, but I have them in a bit of narrow border that is backed by shrubs and is kept constantly enriched. A groundwork of the large-leaved form of megasea cordifolia is planted so as to surround variously sized groups of begonias — groups of from five to nine plants. The setting of the more solid leaves gives the begonias a better

"A groundwork of the large-leaved form of megasea cordifolia is planted so as to surround variously sized groups of begonias".

appearance and makes their bright bloom tell more vividly. They follow in this sequence of colouring: yellow, white, palest pink, full pink, rose, deep red, deep rose, salmon-rose, red-lead colour or orange-scarlet, scarlet, red-lead and orange.

The rock garden

Now is the moment to get to work on the rock garden; there is no time of year so precious for this work as September. Small things planted now, while the ground is still warm, grow at the root at once, and get both anchor-hold and feeding-hold of the ground before frost comes ... and when the first spring warmth comes they can draw upon the reserve of strength they have been hoarding up, and make good growth at once.

A destructive storm

The fierce gales and heavy rains of the last days of September wrought sad havoc among the flowers... If anything about a garden could be disheartening, it would be its aspect after such a storm of wind. Wall shrubs, only lately made safe, as we thought, have great gaps torn out of them, though tied with tarred string to strong iron staples, staples and all being wrenched out. Everything looks battered, and whipped, and ashamed; branches of trees and shrubs lie about far from their sources of origin; green leaves and little twigs are washed up into thick drifts; apples and quinces, that should have hung till mid-October, lie bruised and muddy under the trees. Newly-planted roses and hollies have a funnel-shaped hole worked in the ground at their base, showing the power of the wind to twist their heads, and giving warning of a corresponding disturbance of the tender roots. There is nothing to be done but to look round carefully and search out all the disasters and repair them as well as may be, and to sweep up the wreckage and rubbish, and try to forget the rough weather, and enjoy the calm beauty of the better days that follow, and hope that it may be long before such another angry storm is sent. And indeed a few quiet days of sunshine and mild temperature work wonders. In a week one would hardly know that the garden had been so cruelly torn about. Fresh flowers take the place of bruised ones, and wholesome young growths prove the enduring vitality of vegetable life. Still we cannot help feeling, towards the end of September, that the flower year is nearly at an end, though the end is a gorgeous one, with its strong yellow masses of the later perennial sunflowers and marigolds, goldenrod, and a few belated gladioli; the brilliant foliage of Virginian creepers, the leaf-painting of vitis coignettii, and the strong crimson of the claret vine.

*   *   *

The nights are growing chilly, with even a little frost, and the work for the coming season of dividing and transplanting hardy plants has already begun.

"Early in September, when the autumn flowers are at their finest, some of the starworts are in bloom. Even in August they have already begun, with the beautiful low-growing aster acris ... From the time this pretty plant is in bloom to near the end of October, and even later, there is a constant succession of these welcome Michaelmas daisies".
George S. Elgood, "Michaelmas daisies: Munstead Wood".

"In the early autumn, when the flower borders, if not quite done for, are at least at their last stage before final dissolution, it is a joy to come upon a well-planted border of Michaelmas daisies..."

"...with their clear fresh colouring all the more accentuated by contrast with the general sombre rustiness of the greater part of the neighbouring vegetation. For the extension of the time of enjoyment of hardy flowers, as well as for their own beauty, it is well worth while to have them in a separate border".

Michaelmas daisies

The early days of October bring with them the best bloom of the Michaelmas daisies, the many beautiful garden kinds of the perennial aster. They have, as they well deserve to have, a garden to themselves. Passing along the wide path in front of the big flower border, and through the pergola that forms its continuation, with eye and brain full of rich, warm colouring of flower and leaf, it is a delightful surprise to pass through the pergola's last right-hand opening, and to come suddenly upon the Michaelmas daisy garden in full beauty. Its clean, fresh, pure colouring, of pale and dark lilac, strong purple, and pure white, among masses of pale-green foliage, forms a contrast almost startling after the warm colouring of nearly everything else; and the sight of a region where the flowers are fresh and newly opened, and in glad spring-like profusion, when all else is on the verge of death and decay, gives an impression of satisfying refreshment that is hardly to be equalled throughout the year.

"A September grey garden . . . seen at its best by reaching it through the orange borders . . . This filling with the strong, rich colouring has the natural effect of making the eye eagerly desirous for the complementary colour, so that, by . . . suddenly turning to look into the grey garden, the effect is surprisingly — quite astonishingly — luminous and refreshing".

Autumn colouring

The bracken in the copse stands dry and dead, but when leaves are fluttering down and the chilly days of mid-October are upon us, its warm, rusty colouring is certainly cheering; the green of the freshly grown mossy carpet below looks vividly bright by contrast. Some bushes of spindle-tree (euonymus europæus) are loaded with their rosy seed-pods; some are already burst, and show the orange-scarlet seeds — an audacity of colouring that looks all the brighter for the even, lustreless green of the leaves and of the green-barked twigs and stems.

Autumn planting

During the year I make careful notes of any trees or shrubs that will be wanted, either to come from the nursery or to be transplanted within my own ground, so as to plant them as early as possible. Of the two extremes it is better to plant too early than too late. I would rather plant deciduous trees before the leaves are off than wait till after Christmas, but of all planting times the best is from the middle of October till the end of November, and the same time is the best for all hardy plants of large or moderate size.

I have no patience with slovenly planting. I like to have the ground prepared some months in advance, and when the proper time comes, to do the actual planting as well as possible. The hole in the already prepared ground is taken out so that the tree shall stand exactly right for depth, though in dry soil it is well to make the hole an inch or two deeper, in order to leave the tree standing in the centre of a shallow depression, to allow of a good watering now and then during the following summer. The hole must be made wide enough to give easy space for the most outward-reaching of the roots; they must be spread out on all sides, carefully combing them out with the fingers, so that they all lay out to the best advantage. Any roots that have been bruised, or have broken or jagged ends, are cut off with a sharp knife on the homeward side of the injury. Most gardeners when they plant, after the first spadeful or two has been thrown over the root, shake the bush with an up and down joggling movement. This is useful in the case of plants with a good lot of bushy root, such as berberis, helping to get the grains of earth well in among the root; but in tree planting, where the roots are laid out flat, it is of course useless.

October flowers

Towards the end of October outdoor flowers in anything like quantity cannot be expected, and yet there are patches of bloom here and there in nearly every corner of the garden. The pretty Mediterranean periwinkle (vinca acutiflora) is in full bloom. As with many another southern plant that in its own home likes a cool and shady place, it prefers a sunny one in our latitude. The flowers are of a pale and delicate grey-blue colour, nearly as large as those of the common vinca major, but they are borne more generously as to numbers on radical shoots that form thick, healthy-looking tufts of polished green foliage. It is not very common in gardens, but distinctly desirable.

In the bulb-beds the bright yellow sternbergia lutea is in flower. At first sight it looks something like a crocus of unusually firm and solid substance; but it is an amaryllis, and its pure and even yellow colouring is quite unlike that of any of the crocuses. The numerous upright leaves are thick, deep green, and glossy. It flowers rather shyly in our poor soil, even in well-made beds, doing much better in chalky ground.

Czar violets are giving their fine and fragrant flowers on stalks nine inches long. To have them at their best they must be carefully cultivated and liberally enriched. No plants answer better to good treatment, or spoil more quickly by neglect. A miserable sight is a forgotten violet-bed where they have run together into a tight mat, giving only few and poor flowers. I have seen the owner of such a bed stand over it and blame the plants, when he should have laid the lash on his own shoulders... The Czar are slightly hardier than the newer and larger varieties, but all are thankful for a little shelter from frost.

The hardy flower border

As soon as may be in November the big hardy flower-border has to be thoroughly looked over. The first thing is to take away all "soft stuff". This includes all dead annuals and biennials and any tender things that have been put in for the summer, also Paris daisies, zinnias, French and African marigolds, helichrysums, mulleins, and a few geraniums.

*   *   *

*"Groups of anemone
japonica ... are spreading
beyond bounds
and must be reduced"*.

The dahlias are now cut down and dug up from the border and others collected from different parts of the garden. The labels are tied on to the short stumps that remain, and the roots are laid for a time on the floor of a shed. If the weather has been rainy just before taking them up, it is well to lay them upside down, so that any wet there may be about the bases of the large hollow stalks may drain out. They are left for perhaps a fortnight without shaking out the earth that holds between the tubers, so that they may be fairly dry before they are put away for the winter in a cellar.

Dividing plants

Then we go back to the flower border and dig out all the plants that have to be divided every year. It will also be the turn for some others that only want division every two or three or more years, as the case may be. First, out come all the perennial sunflowers. These divide themselves into two classes; those whose roots make close clumpy masses, and those that throw out long stolons ending in a blunt snout, which is the growing crown for next year.

*　　*　　*

Phloxes must also be taken up. They are always difficult here, unless the season is unusually rainy; in dry summers, even with mulching and watering, I cannot keep them from drying up. The outside pieces are cut off and the woody middle thrown away. It is surprising what a tiny bit of phlox will make a strong flowering plant in one season... I do not have many Michaelmas daisies in the flower border, only some early ones that flower within September... These of course come up, and any patches of gladiolus are collected, to be dried for a time and then stored.

The next thing is to look through the border for the plants that require occasional renewal. In the front I find that a longish patch of heuchera Richardsoni has about half the plants overgrown. These must come up, and are cut to pieces. It is not a nice plant to divide; it has strong middle crowns, and though there are many side ones, they are attached to the main ones too high up to have roots of their own; but I boldly slice down the main stocky stem with straight downward cuts, so as to give a piece of the thick stock to each side bit.

*　　*　　*

A plasterer's hammer is a tool that is very handy for dividing plants. It has a hammer on one side of the head, and a cutting blade like a small chopper on the other. With this and a cold chisel and a strong knife one can divide any roots in comfort. I never divide things by brutally chopping them across with a spade. Plants that have soft fleshy tubers like dahlias and paeonies want the cold chisel; it can be cleverly inserted among the crowns so that injury to the tubers is avoided, and it is equally useful in the case of some plants whose points of attachment are almost as hard as wire, like orobus vernus, or as tough as a door-mat, like iris graminia.

November flowers

The giant Christmas rose (helleborus maximus) is in full flower; it is earlier than the true Christmas rose, being at its best by the middle of November. It is a large and massive flower, but compared with the later kinds has a rather coarse look. The bud and the back of the flower are rather heavily tinged with a dull pink, and it never has the pure-white colouring throughout of the later ones.

I have taken some pains to get together some really hardy November-blooming chrysanthemums. The best of all is a kind frequent in neighbouring cottage-gardens, and known hereabouts as Cottage Pink... Its place is in the open garden; if against a south or west wall, so much the better. Perhaps one year in seven the bloom may be spoilt by a severe frost, but it will bear unharmed several degrees of frost and much rain. I know no chrysanthemum of so true a pink colour, the colour deepening to almost crimson in the centre. After the first frost the foliage of this kind turns to a splendid colour, the green of the leaves giving place to a rich crimson that sometimes clouds the outer portion of the leaf, and often covers its whole expanse. The stiff, wholesome foliage adds much to the beauty of the outdoor kinds, contrasting most agreeably with the limp, mildewed leafage of those indoors.

Autumn roses

Roses are with us for six months out of the twelve; as bushes large and small, as trim standards, as arbour and pergola coverings, as wall plants, as great natural fountains, and as far-reaching rambling growths rushing through thickets and up trees and tossing out their flower-laden sprays from quite unexpected heights. But of all the roses of the year I think there are none more truly welcome than those of autumn.

"Of all the roses of the year I think there are none more truly welcome than those of autumn ... The long-branching teas, that one can cut of lavish length, and especially the noisettes, are always faithful in the quantity and persistence of their autumn bloom".

"Most trusty of all is climbing Aimée Vibert, with its wide-spread terminal clusters of charming warm-white flower and rose-edged bud".

The long-branching teas, that one can cut of lavish length, and especially the noisettes, are always faithful in the quantity and persistence of their autumn bloom. From the end of August to the end of September, sometimes even later, one can enjoy these lovely things in quantity. Most trusty of all is climbing Aimée Vibert, with its wide-spread terminal clusters of charming warm-white flower and rose-edged bud. The flowers of Madame Alfred Carrière, another white rose, are also in plenty; large and loose and of a warm-white colour impossible to describe, but that may sometimes be seen in some shell of delicate structure. No rose of all the year is lovelier in water in a loose long-stalked bunch; the pale polished leaves being also of much beauty.

* * *

It should not be forgotten that some roses are in fact evergreens; retaining all or part of their foliage throughout the winter. One would expect this in the rambling cluster roses that have their origin in rosa sempervirens, but I do not know what parentage accounts for the splendid winter leafage of that grand rambling Reine Olga de Wurtemburg, whose half-double flowers of a fine crimson colour, of great beauty in the half-opened bud state, gladden us throughout the summer, and whose large and healthy deep-green leaves, on yearling shoots fifteen feet long, remain in perfection till long after Christmas.

Sheltering tender plants and shrubs

The first really frosty day we go to the upper part of the wood and cut out from among the many young Scotch firs as many as we think will be wanted for sheltering plants and shrubs of doubtful hardiness. One section of the high wall at the back of the flower border is planted with rather tender things, so that the whole is covered with sheltering fir-boughs.

* * *

Some large hydrangeas in tubs are moved to a sheltered place and put close together, a mound of sand being shovelled up all round to nearly the depth of the tubs; then a wall is made of thatched hurdles, and dry fern is packed well in among the heads of the plants. They would be better in a frost-proof shed, but we have no such place to spare.

* * *

In a cottage garden I learnt a useful lesson in protecting plants, namely, the use of thickly-cut peaty sods. The goodwife had noticed that the peaty ground of the adjoining common, covered with heath and gorse and mossy grass, resisted frost much better than the garden or meadow, and it had been her practice for many years to get some thick dry sods with the heath left on and to pack them close round to protect tender plants. In this way she had preserved her fuchsias of greenhouse kinds, and calceolarias.

Collecting and mulching fallen leaves

Now, in the third week of November, the most pressing work is the collecting of leaves for mulching and leaf-mould. The oaks have been late in shedding their leaves, and we have been waiting till they are down. Oak-leaves are the best, then hazel, elm, and Spanish chestnut. Birch and beech are not so good; beech-leaves especially take much too long to decay. This is, no doubt, the reason why nothing grows willingly under beeches... The leaves are trodden down close and covered with a layer of mould, in which winter salad stuff is immediately planted. The mass of leaves will soon begin to heat, and will give a pleasant bottom heat throughout the winter. Other loads of leaves go into an open pen about ten feet square and five feet deep. Two such pens, made of stout oak post and rail and upright slabs, stand side by side in the garden yard. The one newly filled has just been emptied of its two-year-old leaf-mould, which has gone as a nourishing and protecting mulch over beds of daffodils and choice bulbs and alströmerias, some being put aside in reserve for potting and various uses. The other pen remains full of the leaves of last year, slowly rotting into wholesome plant-food.

"Leaves go into an open pen about ten feet square and five feet deep. Two such pens, made of stout oak post and rail and upright slabs, stand side by side in the garden yard".

Thinning in the copse

Some thinning of birch-trees has to be done in the lowest part of the copse, not far from the house. They are rather evenly distributed on the ground, and I wish to get them into groups by cutting away superfluous trees. On the neighbouring moorland and heathy uplands they are apt to grow naturally in groups, the individual trees generally bending outward towards the free, open space, the whole group taking a form that is graceful and highly pictorial. I hope to be able to cut out trees so as to leave the remainder standing in some such way. But as a tree once cut cannot be put up again, the condemned ones are marked with bands of white paper right around the trunks, so that they can be observed from all sides, thus to give a chance of reprieve to any tree that from any point of view may have pictorial value.

The winter aspect

The leaves are all down by the last week of November, and woodland assumes its winter aspect; perhaps one ought rather to say, some one of its infinite variety of aspects, for those who live in such country know how many are the winter moods of forest land, and how endless are its variations of atmospheric effect and pictorial beauty — variations much greater and more numerous than are possible in summer.

With the wind in the south-west and soft rain about, the twigs of the birches look almost crimson, while the dead bracken at their foot, half-draggled and sodden with wet, is of a strong, dark rust colour. Now one sees the full value of the good evergreens, and, rambling through woodland, more especially of the holly, whether in bush or tree form, with its masses of strong green colour, dark and yet never gloomy. Whether it is the high polish of the leaves, or the lively look of their wavy edges, with the short prickles set alternately up and down, or the brave way the tree has of shooting up among other thick growth, or its massive sturdiness on a bare hillside, one cannot say, but a holly in early winter, even without berries, is always a cheering sight. John Evelyn is eloquent in his praise of this grand evergreen, and lays special emphasis on this quality of cheerfulness.

Near my home is a little wild valley, whose planting, wholly done by nature, I have all my life regarded with admiration.

The arable fields of an upland farm give place to hazel copses as the ground rises. Through one of these a deep narrow lane ... leads by a rather sudden turn into the lower end of the little valley. Its grassy bottom is only a few yards wide, and its sides rise steeply right and left. Looking upward through groups of wild bushes and small trees, one sees thickly-wooded ground on the higher levels... On the steeply-rising banks are large groups of juniper, some tall, some spreading, some laced and wreathed about with tangles of honeysuckle, now in brown winter dress, and there are a few bushes of spindle tree, whose green stems and twigs look strangely green in winter. Thorns stand some singly, some in close companionship, impenetrable masses of short-twigged prickly growth, with here and there a wild rose shooting straight up through the crowded branches. One thinks how lovely it will be in early June, when the pink rose-wreaths are tossing out of the foamy sea of white thorn blossom. Hollies are towering masses of health and vigour. Some of the groups of thorn and holly are intermingled; all show beautiful arrangements of form and colour, such as are never seen in planted places... So the narrow track leads on, showing the same kinds of tree and bush in endless variety of beautiful grouping, under the sombre half-light of the winter day. It is afternoon, and as one mounts higher a pale bar of yellow light gleams between the farther tree-stems, but all above is grey with angry blackish drifts of ragged wrack... To the left is broken ground and a steep-sided hill, towards whose shoulder the track rises... Now I look into the ruddy heads of the thorns, bark and fruit both of rich warm colouring, and into the upper masses of the hollies, also reddening into wealth of berry.

"September is the month of dahlias and of several other kinds of flowers that tend to large size and bold aspect. As a cut flower the worst feature of the dahlia is its foliage; it is heavy in colour, uninteresting in form, and dull in texture. In my own practice I avoid using it, preferring to set up the dahlias, if on long stalks, with leafage that I think is more interesting, and giving them a softening accompaniment of clematis flammula ... Another way of using dahlias is to arrange them with shorter stalks in some large shallow vessel, sometimes grouping two vessels together; the better to make one large effect. Flower vases are often too much spotted about rooms. Such a simple arrangement of two things grouped together allows of a freer use of material, and often has a much better effect as a room decoration''.

Autumn flowers for decoration

In September and October there are plenty of bold flowers for large arrangements. Hydrangeas go on throughout the autumn and nearly to November. Tiger lilies are fine in rooms; splendid against dark oak with red-leaved branches of the claret vine. Pink and white crinums are beautiful with boldy-cut leaf-spikes of variegated maize; cannas have their own grand foliage; the leaves of Chinese paeonies are in many shades of subdued red that can be used with scarlet and orange dahlias, gladioli, scarlet salvias and orange African marigolds.

*   *   *

The earlier hardy chrysanthemums are some of our best October flowers. Those of red, orange, bronze and bronze-pink colourings arrange well with some of our red bush branches, and the whites and pale yellows with branches of golden privet and Japan honeysuckle, whose veined and gold-splashed leaves are now at their best. White and pink chrysanthemums we put with foliage of cineraria maritima, and white alone either with the dusky grey-green of ilex or the splendid richness of bay.

But the flower-glory of October, with its unending wealth of bloom for cutting, is in the later Michaelmas daisies, of all shades of lilac and purple, white and mauve-pink.

*   *   *

The first fortnight of November is rich in the ample supply of bloom given by the true hardy chrysanthemums. It is only on very rare occasions, that the flower buds are so much crippled that the bloom is spoilt. It may safely be said that in nine Novembers out of ten these capital flowers may be depended on... Another material for room decoration to be looked out for early in November is the long-stalked pods of berries of iris fœtidissima. It is a native plant whose ornamental qualities are often overlooked, but for its vigorous dark green glossy foliage alone it deserves a place in every garden, preferably in half shade, on the cool side of some wall or building.

Autumn berries and foliage in the house

September brings the handsome fruit clusters of mountain ash berries in greater perfection; the fruit of the water elder becomes more transparent and gains greater refinement. The spindle-tree berries are opening their outer coats of rosy pink and showing the orange seeds within. In some seaside places, both on sand and on clay, the sea buckthorn has its grey-leaved branches loaded with deep orange berries. The black bryony of hedge and woodland bears scarlet and green fruit, and the polished heart-shaped leaves have either taken a deeper tint of rich green or turned to a deep red-bronze, almost black.

Fennel, with its pretty yellow umbels and fine hair-like foliage is still in

"When October is here we feel that we must make the most of the flowers that remain ... for at any moment a sharp pinch of frost may come and destroy what is left. So we have great bowls and basins of ... late roses".

"The first fortnight of November is rich in the ample supply of bloom given by the true hardy chrysanthemums ... After slight frosts the foliage of Cottage Pink turns to a fine crimson colour, harmonising well with the crimson centre of the not over-blown flower".

"A September arrangement made of bramble, traveller's joy in fruit, fronds of male fern, a berried trail of black bryony, thistles, a seeding spike of French willow (epilobium), yarrow, mayweed from a stubble field, and an out-of season 'puff' of dandelion".

good bloom; it is effective cut long, with yellowish foliage of oak or ash or Spanish chestnut.

October goes with September for its hedge fruits, and late flowers will be the same, but it has the addition of the beauty of yellowing and red-tinted foliage of which beech, lasting into November, is perhaps the most useful. Often in woodland, where undergrowth has been cut, shoots of green-foliaged oak may be found right up to Christmas. Hawthorn berries hang long after the leaves are gone, giving the whole bushes a pleasant, ruddy look.

"Even before the New Year there will have been bloom on the ever-welcome iris stylosa, with its delicious scent ... There is a clean, smooth look about the flower, trim and fresh in its light blue-purple dress".

"Cyclamen coum, a charming plant for ground cover ... is a short growing plant, scarcely over three inches in height, and has dark crimson flowers and leathery, roundish leaves".

"Muscari botryoides, with its well-filled spikes of bloom and neat leaves carried upright, a distinguishing character in this species".

Green things of the winter garden — Winter flowering plants
A winter garden — Preparing sticks and stakes — Frosts
Small trees and shrubs for winter colour — Winter woodland
Distant promise of summer — Berberis aquifolium — Forms of trees
Winter flowers and foliage for decoration
Winter wild fruits and foliage in the house

Green things of the winter garden

When the leaves are down and the flower borders are bare one turns with a feeling of grateful admiration to the evergreen trees, plants and bushes. They are all the more to be appreciated because so many of them are now in their best and deepest coloured foliage. Holly, yew, bay and box are clothed in a kind of subdued splendour that is not only grateful to the eye but gladdening to the mind... Then all the greys and faint browns and silvery greens of tree-bole and branch, and the thin mist so frequent during the days of early winter, form just the right setting for the deep, rich colouring of the evergreens.

*   *   *

It is only in the depth of winter that we fully appreciate the value of evergreen shrubs and trees. In woodland, in the colder months, there is often nothing green but holly and ivy. It is then that we see what precious things are these two native evergreens; not only beautiful in themselves, but giving evidence of comfortable harbourage to many forms of wild life. So also in gardens, the shrubs with persistent foliage, that in summer passed almost without notice, acquire their full value in winter, and are then in their richest dress... In planting garden spaces against buildings the mistake is often made of having borders of temporary or summer plants only, especially in such places as narrow borders between house wall and terrace walk; but if these are filled in with evergreens, such as laurustinus, rosemary, lavender and berberis ... there is a pleasant sense of permanence and a kind of dignity.

*   *   *

Though jasmine is not strictly evergreen, not only does it hold its leaves till Christmas, but the mass of green stem shows with a general green effect. Some climbing roses have the same quality; Jersey Beauty is now (late in January) not only well clothed with its polished foliage, but is bearing such quantities of red hips in thickish bunches that its whole effect is highly ornamental... Garden ivies are only too numerous, but the very large-leaved hedera dentata and the small marbled caenwood variety are so distinct that they should not be forgotten. Cistus cyprius is a fine thing ... its fragrant foliage turning strangely blue in winter. Shrubs with variegated leaves should be used with caution, to avoid the danger of a patchy effect; but where questions of colour are carefully considered and a harmonious background for flowers of bright yellow colouring is desired, it is well to train on the wall both the gold-splashed elaeagnus and the golden privet.

Winter flowering plants

The earliest flowers to appear are the winter aconite (eranthis hyemalis) and the Christmas roses, varieties of helleborus niger. Though they bloom nearly at the same time, it is better to treat them separately. The little winter aconite is best planted under some deciduous tree in thin woodland, when this comes near the garden; perhaps for preference under the outer branches of a beech, as the yellow blooms and the carpet of rusty leaves come so well together. Christmas roses enjoy a cool place in rich loam where they are never droughted; a quiet dell of their own in a fern garden is a good place.

*   *   *

I never tire of admiring and praising iris stylosa, which has proved itself such a good plant for English gardens; at any rate, for those in our southern counties. Lovely in form and colour, sweetly-scented and with admirable foliage, it has in addition to these merits the unusual one of a blooming season of six months' duration. The first flowers come with the earliest days of November, and its season ends with a rush of bloom in the first half of April... It thrives in rather poor soil, and seems to bloom all the better for having its root-run invaded by some stronger plant. When I first planted a quantity I had brought from its native place, I made the mistake of putting it in a well-prepared border. At first I was delighted to see how well it flourished, but as it gave me only thick masses of leaves a yard long, and no flowers, it was clear that it wanted to be less well fed. After changing it to poor soil, at the foot of a sunny wall close to a strong clump of alströmeria, I was rewarded with a good crop of flowers; and the more the alströmeria grew into it on one side and plumbago larpentœ on the other, the more freely the brave little iris flowered.

"Among some of the best of the small bulbous irises that we can bloom in the open in the earliest months, iris histrioides is of much beauty ... with large flowers which are handsomely blotched on the falls with white and purple".

*   *   *

What a precious winter flower is the yellow jasmine (jasminum nudiflorum). Though hard frost spoils the flowers then expanded, as soon as milder days come the hosts of buds that are awaiting them burst into bloom.

*   *   *

Some of the hardy cyclamens flower in the late autumn, but there are two species that are essentially flowers of spring. C. coum, a native of Asia Minor and Southern Europe, is in bloom in February and March... The leaves... though they are faintly clouded with lighter colour, are wanting in the distinct whitish marbling that is so attractive in the foliage of some of the other species. There is also a good white variety. C. ibericum is a larger plant with better marked leaves and rose-red flowers that have deep red-purple colouring at the base. It is thought by some to deserve specific rank, but botanists consider that it is a form of c. coum. In the open garden the plants should be in a sheltered nook in rockwork where there is thorough drainage, and it is all the better if they can have some kind of overhead protection.

* * *

It is always a delight to see in February the closely packed heads of hyacinthus azureus, quite surprising in their clear brightness of light sky-blue colouring. This class of hyacinth is so closely allied to the muscari and so nearly resembles them in form and general appearance, that they may be considered as one class of bulb for garden purposes. Of the true muscari there are two that stand out as the most desirable. The first is m. botryoides, with its well-filled spikes of bloom and neat leaves carried upright, a distinguishing character in this species. It is in three varieties, all of value, namely, the type (blue-purple), a paler blue-purple, and a capital white. The second is m. conicum, and especially the fine garden variety called Heavenly Blue, a remarkably good garden plant. The foliage has not the brisk, alert carriage of m. botryoides — it is longer and more lax; but when a patch is well established, the mass of large bloom a foot high, of splendid purple-blue, is an arresting sight. These two are by far the best as garden plants.

Left, "The double white anemone hepatica ... is considered a great rarity and is always much prized".

Below, "In our gardens anemone blanda likes a warm bank or sheltered piece of rockwork, where it is an admirable companion to the various kinds of early iris and crocus".

* * *

The race for precedence in time of flowering among the early anemones is between blanda and hepatica; both may be looked for in February. Anemone blanda is a small Greek plant with much the same character as the larger, later and more free growing apennina, but it keeps closer to the ground, the usual height being from three to four inches. The flowers are of a deep blue

*"The winter garden —
a delightful invention! Walled
on all sides, the walling not
high enough to exclude the
low winter sun, it is
absolutely sheltered...
The brick-paved paths
are always dry, and a seat in
a hooded recess is a
veritable sun-trap".*

colour... In cultivation it varies in colour to paler shades of blue and even to white, but none of these are equal in value to the colour of the type. A. hepatica, more commonly called hepatica triloba, is a native of the Alps and Southern Europe. It is a very old favourite in gardens. Parkinson, writing near 1629, describes ten varieties, of which two, a blue and a purple, are double. A double white has appeared from time to time.

A winter garden

How good it would be to have a good space set apart as a hardy winter garden... Such a place would be truly enjoyable from the middle of November and onward all through the winter, besides being a green garden of no little beauty. It would not be entirely without flowers, for in a cool nook near the path there would be the giant Christmas rose early in November, followed by the later-flowering kinds; and in another such place the Lent hellebores blooming at a time when late winter joins hands with earliest spring. These might make a flowery undergrowth for quite a considerable space on the cooler side, while facing them on the sunny aspect there would be tufts of iris stylosa flowering in all open weather throughout the winter months. If a rocky or sandy scarp of a few feet high should be there, the yellow jasmine would find a place, and could be so planted as to fall in sheets over the face of the scarp. There are other possible flowering things, among which the winter heaths should be remembered, but there would be no need to strain for more flowers, for just these few would give enough points of interest, and, with the holly berries, enough of actual bright colouring. In fact, the winter garden is all the better for the fewness of its flowers. The summer garden is only too full of brilliant objects of beauty and interest, and the winter garden should have its own rather contrasting character as a place of comparative repose of mind and eye.

If the winter garden is on a sandy or peaty soil it will perhaps have all the better opportunity, for then many more of the lesser evergreens can be employed, and a part of the middle background would be of rhododendrons. When these are planted they are often considered as flowering shrubs alone, but, fine things though they are when in bloom, the flower is for summer weeks alone. For the rest of the year they are for foliage only, and it is as masses of rich greenery that they serve in the winter garden.

Preparing sticks and stakes

A spell of frosty days at the end of December puts a stop to all planting and ground work. Now we go into the copse and cut the trees that have been provisionally marked, judged, and condemned, with the object of leaving the remainder standing in graceful groups... The best of the birch tops are cut into pea-sticks, a clever, slanting cut with the hand-bill leaving them pointed and ready for use. Throughout the copse are "stools" of Spanish chestnut, cut about once in five years. From this we get good straight stakes for dahlias and hollyhocks, also beanpoles; while the rather straight-branched boughs are cut into branching sticks for Michaelmas daisies, and special lengths are got ready for various kinds of plants — chrysanthemums, lilies, paeonies, and so on. To provide all this in winter, when other work is slack or impossible, is an important matter in the economy of a garden, for all gardeners know how distressing and harassing it is to find themselves without the right sort of sticks or stakes in summer, and what a long job it then seems to have to look them up and cut them, of indifferent quality, out of dry faggots. By the plan of preparing all in winter no precious time is lost, and a tidy withe-bound bundle of the right sort is always at hand. The rest of the rough spray and small branching stuff is made up into faggots to be chopped up for fire-lighting... The middle-sized branches — anything between two inches and six inches in diameter — are what the woodmen call "top and lop"; these are also cut into convenient lengths, and are stacked in the barn, to be cut into billets for next year's fires in any wet or frosty weather, when outdoor work is at a standstill.

Frosts

A hard frost is upon us... One of the yuccas threw up a stout flower-spike. I had thought of protecting and roofing the spike, in the hope of carrying it safely through till spring, but meanwhile there came a damp day and a frosty night, and when I saw it again it was spoilt.

* * *

"Frost on gaultheria shallon foliage ... The thermometer registered eighteen degrees last night, and though there was only one frosty night before it, the ground is hard frozen".

More or less unseasonable weather may be regarded in this country as the rule rather than the exception, and consequently the rosarian is kept in a continual state of anxiety as to what unfavourable climatic changes his favourites may next be called upon to encounter. No doubt one reason for these anxieties is due to the fact that most of our cultivated roses are only half-hardy plants, and therefore peculiarly susceptible to all kinds of unfavourable weather influences [one of which is] frost. This may be divided

"For protecting standard teas ... bracken, cut in September before it has become brittle, should be secured to the heads; or a more effectual protection may be afforded by first drawing the shoots of the plant together and then lightly thatching the head with straw or bracken fastened above it to a firm stake".

into two classes — the winter frosts and the spring frosts. Against the former the protection provided cannot well be too complete, whereas very moderate means will mostly be sufficient to ward off injuries from spring frosts; and yet against the ill effects of these spring frosts there is practically no remedy, unless it be syringeing or spraying the frosted foliage with water very early in the morning in order to thaw it before sunrise. For at that season it is not so much the damage done by the frost itself that has to be guarded against as the sudden thawing of the frozen leaves by the sun shining on them. Of course the reason why spring frosts are so difficult to deal with as compared with winter frosts is that in the one case the plants are clothed with delicate young foliage, whereas in the winter it is only necessary to protect the lower portion of the leafless shoots.

Small trees and shrubs for winter colour

The cardinal willow has bright red bark, salix britzensis orange, and the golden osier bright yellow. The yearly growth has the best-coloured bark, so that when they are employed for giving colour it is usual to cut them every winter; moreover, the large quantity of young shoots that the cutting induces naturally increases the density of the colour effect. But if they are planted in a rather large way it is better that the regular winter cutting should be restricted to those near the outer edge, and to let a good proportion of those within stand for two or more years, and to have some in the background that are never cut at all, but that are allowed to grow to their full size and to show their natural habit.

It will also be well, instead of planting them exclusively sort by sort, to group and intergroup carefully assorted colours, such as the scarlet willow with the purple-barked kind, and to let this pass into the American willow with the black stem. Such a group should not be too large, and it should be near the pathway, for it will show best near at hand. For the sake of the bark-colouring, it would be best to cut it all every year, although in the larger plantings it is desirable to have the trees of different ages, or the effect may be too much that of a mere crop instead of a well-arranged garden grouping.

Some of the garden roses, both of the free-growing and bush kinds, have finely coloured bark that can be used in much the same way ... Of the free kinds, the best coloured are rosa ferruginea, whose leaves are red as well as the stem — it is the rosa rubrifolia of nurseries — and the varieties of Boursault roses, derived from rosa alpina. As bushes for giving reddish colouring, rosa lucida would be among the best.

*   *   *

Some shrubs have conspicuously green bark, such as the spindle-tree; but the habit of growth is rather too diffuse to let it make a distinct show of colour. Leycesteria formosa is being tried in mass for winter colour in some gardens, but I venture to feel a little doubtful of its success; for though the skin of the half-woody stem is bright green, the plant has the habit of retaining some of its leaves and the remains of its flowering tips till January, or even later. After frost these have the appearance of untidy grey rags, and are distinctly unsightly. The brightest effect of all green-barked plants is that given by whortleberry, a plant that on peaty or sandy soils is one of the most enjoyable of winter undershrubs.

Winter woodland

The ground has a warm carpet of pale rusty fern; tree-stem and branch and twig show tender colour-harmonies of grey bark and silver-grey lichen, only varied by the warm feathery masses of birch spray. Now the splendid richness of the common holly is more than ever impressive, with its solid masses of full, deep colour, and its wholesome look of perfect health and vigour. Sombrely cheerful, if one may use such a mixture of terms; sombre by reason of the extreme depth of tone, and yet cheerful from the look of glad life, and from the assurance of warm shelter and protecting comfort to bird and beast and neighbouring vegetation. The picture is made complete by the slender shafts of the silver-barked birches, with their half-weeping heads of delicate, warm-coloured spray. Has any tree so graceful a way of throwing up its stems as the birch? They seem to leap and spring into the air, often leaning and curving upward from the very root, sometimes in forms that would be almost grotesque were it not for the never-failing rightness of free-swinging poise and perfect balance. The tints of the stem give a precious lesson in colour. The white of the bark is here silvery-white and there milk-white, and sometimes shows the faintest tinge of rosy flush. Where the bark has not yet peeled, the stem is clouded and banded with delicate grey, and with the silver-green of lichen.

Distant promise of summer

There is always in February some one day, at least, when one smells the yet distant, but surely coming, summer. Perhaps it is a warm, mossy scent that greets one when passing along the southern side of a hedge-bank; or it may be in some woodland opening, where the sun has coaxed out the pungent smell of the trailing ground ivy, whose blue flowers will soon appear; but the day always comes, and with it the glad certainty that summer is nearing, and that the good things promised will never fail.

How strangely little of positive green colour is to be seen in copse and woodland. Only the moss is really green. The next greenest thing is the northern sides of the trunks of beech and oak. Walking southward they are all green, but looking back they are silver-grey. The undergrowth is of brambles and sparse fronds of withered bracken; the bracken less beaten down than usual, for the winter has been without snow; only where the soil is deeper, and the fern has grown more tall and rank, it has fallen into thick, almost felted masses, and the stalks all lying one way make the heaps look like lumps of fallen thatch. The bramble leaves — last year's leaves, which are held all the winter — are of a dark, brackish-bronze colour, or nearly red where they have seen the sun. Age seems to give them a sort of hard surface and enough of a polish to reflect the sky; the young leaves that will come next month are almost woolly at first. Grassy tufts show only bleached bents, so tightly matted that one wonders how the delicate young blades will be able to spear through. Ivy berries, hanging in thick clusters, are still in beauty; they are so heavy that they weigh down the branches.

Berberis aquifolium

Berberis aquifolium begins to colour after the first frosts; though some plants remain green, the greater number take on some rich tinting of red or purple, and occasionally in poor soil and in full sun a bright red that may almost be called scarlet.

What a precious thing this fine old berberis is! What should we do in winter without its vigorous masses of grand foliage in garden and shrubbery, to say nothing of its use indoors? Frequent as it is in gardens, it is seldom used as well or thoughtfully as it deserves. There are many places where, between garden and wood, a well-considered planting of berberis, combined with two or three other things of larger stature, such as the fruiting barberry, and whitethorn and holly, would make a very enjoyable piece of shrub wild-gardening. When one reflects that berberis aquifolium is individually one of the handsomest of small shrubs, that it is at its very best in mid-winter, that every leaf is a marvel of beautiful drawing and construction, and that its ruddy winter colouring is a joy to see, enhanced as it is by the glistening brightness of the leaf-surface; and further, when one remembers that in spring the whole picture changes — that the polished leaves are green again, and the bushes are full of tufted masses of brightest yellow bloom, and fuller of bee-music than any other plant then in flower; and that even then it has another season of beauty yet to come, when in the days of middle summer it is heavily loaded with the thick-clustered masses of berries, covered with a brighter and bluer bloom than almost any other fruit can show — when one thinks of all this brought together in one plant, it seems but right that we should spare no pains to use it well. It is the only hardy shrub I can think of that is in one or other of its varied forms of beauty throughout the year.

Forms of trees

In summer time one never really knows how beautiful are the forms of the deciduous trees. It is only in winter, when they are bare of leaves, that one can fully enjoy their splendid structure and design, their admirable qualities of duly apportioned strength and grace of poise, and the way the spread of the many-branched head has its equivalent in the wide-reaching ground-grasp of the root. And it is interesting to see how, in the many different kinds of tree, the same laws are always in force, and the same results occur, and yet by the employment of what varied means. For nothing in the growth of trees can be much more unlike than the habit of the oak and that of the weeping willow, though the unlikeness only comes from the different adjustment of the same sources of power and the same weights, just as in the movement of wind-blown leaves some flutter and some undulate, while others turn over

"In February beautiful colouring is to be seen in many of the plants whose leaves do not die down in winter. Foremost amongst these is the foam flower (tiarella cordifolia). Its leaves, now lying on the ground, show bright colouring, inclining to scarlet, crimson, and orange".

and back again. Old apple-trees are specially noticeable for their beauty in winter, when their extremely graceful shape, less visible when in loveliness of spring bloom or in rich bounty of autumn fruit, is seen to fullest advantage.

"Snow came on early in the evening [December 1886] . . . when the thermometer was barely at freezing point and there was no wind. It hung on the trees in clogging masses, with a lowering temperature that was soon below freezing. The snow still falling loaded them more and more; then came the fatal wind, and all through that night we heard the breaking trees. When morning came there were eighteen inches of snow on the ground, and all the trees that could be seen, mostly Scotch fir, seemed to be completely wrecked. Some were entirely stripped of branches, and stood up bare, like scaffold poles".

Winter flowers and foliage for decoration

Even in the depth of winter, when flowers are least plentiful, good room decoration may be done with but very few, or indeed with foliage only.

In an average garden that is not quite new, there is always something to be found. A country house is hardly ever without its masses of shrubbery. More than once it has happened that the mistress of such a house bewailed herself to the writer, that there was nothing pickable in the garden; whereas the old shrubberies were simply unworked mines of endless wealth... First there was an old, over-grown aucuba in a shady place among tall shrubs. Its rather pale green leaves were large and wide, and its branches were flung abroad in a way that would evidently suit a large jar of Italian majolica, that my hostess wished to fill with something worthy.

*   *   *

A little further was a batch of berberis; some of it finely coloured. It was easy to choose some straggling pieces nearly three feet long, with good tops of different outward inclination; some nearly upright, and others bending to right and left; and a good branching piece for the middle. Then, greatest prize of all, against a garden shed, was an old bush of the yellow-bloomed winter jasmine (jasminum nudiflorum) in full flower. Some large and long

"Even in the depth of winter, when flowers are least plentiful, good room decoration may be done with but a few ... Christmas rose, laurustinus and foliage of megasea in a Munstead glass".

branches with their pendulous front sprays were soon cut, to be arranged with the berberis.

By now we were fully loaded, but we had to stop again to examine an old tree of golden holly. A search among the lower branches produced what was hoped for — some small twigs whose leaves were pale yellow all over: — "These will be charming in one of your silver bowls with just a few white flowers, Christmas roses or small white hyacinths".

It may safely be said that a raid in any old shrubbery will produce not necessarily exactly this — but enough material of like utility, such as, eked out with a very few flowers, will suffice for satisfactory room decoration.

* * *

There are several shrubs with variegated foliage that are of great use in winter decorations. One of the best of these is the gold-variegated privet, holding its leaves till well after Christmas; a worthy companion to the winter yellow jasmine and any white flowers. The variegated elæagnus is also a capital thing; the branches and twigs are extremely stiff-wooded, and when they are arranged they form a strong scaffolding for the introduction and support of any flowers that are to go with them... The gold-variegated euonymus, both narrow and broad-leaved, is also of much value for winter cutting.

* * *

In January and February there will be the deliciously sweet flowers of the winter-sweet (chimonanthus fragrans). To get the best yield of bloom the shrubs should be pruned hard to short spur-like growths. It is not convenient to cut it in sprays, but the little half-transparent yellowish blooms are picked straight off the wood and floated in shallow dishes.

Winter wild fruits and foliage in the house

Even in winter there is hardly a country district where woodland and hedge-row will not provide something worth bringing home. There are berried boughs of ivy, and, for those who know where to look for them, fronds of polypody and harts tongue ferns, and there are wild rose hips, and foliage of bramble in its red-bronze and sometimes nearly scarlet colouring. Then there are sheets of brilliant mosses, and on hedgebanks little creeping sprays of small-leaved ivy in much variety of colour; some grey-green with white veins, some approaching scarlet where the soil is sandy and the sun has been upon them. These mosses and small ivies alone are charming in flat dishes, and all the more enjoyable because wild flowers there are none and garden flowers scarce, and the mind is not distracted from the quiet loveliness of the few small things that reward the winter quest.

Still our bramble branches are not to be called small things, for we may have them as big as we please. Then when arranged, we see what a beautiful growth is that of our common blackberry — second only in form and freedom to the vine, and not unlike it in its ways and aspect.

"Even in middle winter one can make green foliage groups without flowers that are worthy room-ornaments, for there are always sprays of green ivy to be found and fronds of harts tongue and polypody ferns".

Then in February there are the little scarlet fairy-cups, delicious things to put in a setting of fresh green moss. One hardly knows how strong and cheering are these little jewels of winter scarlet, or how brilliant is the green of winter moss, till one has put the two together. The fairy-cups will be found in hedge-banks where there are trees; they grow on little pieces of decayed wood, generally under elms.

167

COLOUR ILLUSTRATIONS

Acknowledgements are due to the following for kindly allowing us to reproduce the colour illustrations in this anthology

Chris Beetles Ltd., 104 Randolph Avenue, London W9
Pages 17, 25, 29, 36, 40-41, 48, 65, 97, 104-105

Simon Carter Gallery, 23 Market Hill, Woodbridge, Suffolk
Pages 7, 101

Christie's, 8 King Street, St. James's, London SW1
Pages 6, 32, 37, 69, 72

Robert Douwma (Prints & Maps) Ltd., 4 Henrietta Street, Covent Garden, London WC2
Pages 77, 100

Fine-Lines (Fine Art), The Old Rectory, Sheep Street, Shipston-on-Stour, Warwickshire
Frontispiece, pages 3, 14, 45

The Priory Gallery, Station Road, Bishops Cleeve, Nr. Cheltenham, Gloucestershire
Pages 10 (top), 11, 15, 80

Christopher Wood Gallery, 15 Motcomb Street, London SW1
Pages 20, 76, 109, 136-137

The colour illustrations (and in some cases accompanying text) on the following pages have been reproduced from *Some English Gardens*, after drawings by George S. Elgood, R.I., with notes by Gertrude Jekyll, published by Longmans Green & Co., 1904: pages 21, 24, 28, 33, 68, 73, 108, 112, 129, 132, 133, 140, 141, 144

*The extracts in this
anthology of
Gertrude Jekyll's writings
have been taken from the books
illustrated on the right.
All of them are available from the
Antique Collectors' Club*

For further details of these, and other
works on gardening and architecture,
please write to the
Antique Collectors' Club
5 Church Street, Woodbridge, Suffolk, England

The Antique Collectors' Club

WOOD AND GARDEN
GERTRUDE JEKYLL

GARDENS FOR SMALL COUNTRY HOUSES
GERTRUDE JEKYLL & LAWRENCE WEAVER

HOME AND GARDEN
GERTRUDE JEKYLL

FLOWER DECORATION
IN THE HOUSE
GERTRUDE JEKYLL

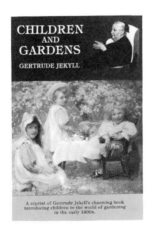

CHILDREN AND GARDENS
GERTRUDE JEKYLL

A reprint of Gertrude Jekyll's charming book introducing children to the world of gardening in the early 1900s.

LILIES FOR ENGLISH GARDENS
GERTRUDE JEKYLL

WALL, WATER AND WOODLAND GARDENS
GERTRUDE JEKYLL

COLOUR SCHEMES FOR THE FLOWER GARDEN
GERTRUDE JEKYLL

ROSES FOR ENGLISH GARDENS
GERTRUDE JEKYLL

A GARDENER'S TESTAMENT
GERTRUDE JEKYLL